JESUS' ALTERNATIVE PLAN

JESUS' ALTERNATIVE PLAN
The Sermon on the Mount

RICHARD ROHR

franciscan
media®
Cincinnati, Ohio

Scripture passages are the author's own paraphrase or his choice from several translations, particularly *The Jerusalem Bible.*

Excerpts from *The Historical Jesus: The Life of a Mediterranean Jewish Peasant*, by John Dominic Crossan, copyright ©1991 by John Dominic Crossan, are reprinted with permission of Harper San Francisco.

The excerpt from *Hidden Women of the Gospels*, copyright © 1996 by Kathy Coffey, published by Crossroad Publishing Company, is reprinted by permission of the publisher.

Cover and book design by Mark Sullivan
Cosmic Egg illustration by Nelson Kane

LIBRARY OF CONGRESS CATALOGING-IN-PUBLICATION DATA
Names: Rohr, Richard, author.
Title: Jesus' alternative plan : the Sermon on the mount / Richard Rohr.
Other titles: Jesus' plan for a new world
Description: Second edition. | Cincinnati, Ohio : Franciscan Media, [2022]
  | Includes bibliographical references. | Summary: "When Jesus talked
  about the Kingdom of God, he was talking about an utterly different way
  of relating to human society as we know it. Richard Rohr takes readers
  through a analysis of the Sermon on Mount to show how this plan applies
  to the 21st century"-- Provided by publisher.
Identifiers: LCCN 2022012964 | ISBN 9781632534163 | ISBN 9781632534170
  (epub)
Subjects: LCSH: Sermon on the mount--Criticism, interpretation, etc.
Classification: LCC BT380.3 .R64 2022 | DDC 226.9/06--dc23/eng/20220412
LC record available at https://lccn.loc.gov/2022012964

ISBN 978-1-63253-416-3

Published by Franciscan Media
28 W. Liberty Street
Cincinnati, OH 45202-6498
www.FranciscanMedia.org

Printed in the United States of America

In memory of my sister Carol, and in gratitude for my sister Alana, and my brother Tim, who kept the home fires burning and supported me in kindling other fires. —RICHARD ROHR, OFM

acknowledgments

I would like to thank my confreres and friends at Franciscan Media, who have continued to trust and support my attempts to communicate the Gospel.

contents

We know everything today
and believe almost nothing.

It is not reason that drives our lives,
but passion or the search for it.
It is not words and concepts,
but living images that grab our souls.
It is not what we know that haunts us at the end,
but what we did not know and don't know yet.

We must make friends with the unknowing.
What you know is just ten thousand different things.

But what you believe
is what you pay attention to,
what you care about,
what finally lives and matters in you.

What you believe is not one of ten thousand things,
it is that which sees ten thousand things.

It is not what you know that matters,
or changes anything:
It is what you believe—
and believe all the way through.

How to Read the Bible

The Bible is the most controversial book in print. It has done an immense amount of good. At the same time, it probably has caused more damage than any other book in human history. That may seem like a shocking statement from a Franciscan, a Catholic priest, but if we look at history, we can see how many Christians acted in oppressive, senseless, and rigid ways in the name of Jesus and the Gospel. That's because they didn't really understand what Jesus was up to.

Thank God that the Roman Catholic Church is encouraging the type of scholarship and theological study that really addresses the Christian Scriptures as the word of God, *written in human history, during a particular time and place.* Through this scholarship, we're trying to be more honest with the Bible, rather than making it say what we want it to say, what we are culturally conditioned to think or need it to say. We are beginning to understand the social, cultural, political, and economic situation in which it was first written.

Not surprisingly, we're finding that a lot of the issues in the Christian Scriptures are eternal issues. (This is, of course, true for the Hebrew Scriptures as well.) But we create incredible misunderstanding by reading and interpreting the text without understanding its context. By digging into the work of understanding Jesus and his times, we find the Christian Scriptures to be a far richer source of spiritual life than we could ever have imagined.

This book is about Jesus' Sermon on the Mount, considered the blueprint for the Christian lifestyle. The secret to understanding the Sermon on the Mount is to understand what Jesus intended when he preached it. So, this book is as much about getting ready to hear the Sermon as it is about the Sermon itself. We'll be skipping all over the Gospel of Matthew and touching on what modern scholars are saying about Jesus' public ministry.

I have intentionally chosen throughout the book to say, "Jesus said." I am aware that the words in print may be from the evangelist, either the memory of a community thirty or more years later or the theological construct of a faith community. But, for me, all that is precisely the *living message of Jesus* we need to hear. Once we're ready to hear the Sermon, it requires very little explanation. That will become clearer in the first chapters of this book.

One of the problems in reading the Bible is that most of us Christians preconceive Jesus as "the divine savior of our divine church," which prematurely settles all the dust and struggle. Such a predisposition does not open us to enlightenment by Christ, but, in fact, deadens and numbs our perception. A part of us reads the Bible in order to prove this understanding of Jesus. He's God of our saved church, which means that our church is right—and so are we. If we are honest enough to admit that bias, we may have a chance of letting go of it for a richer understanding of the Gospel.

We bring our hearts to reading the Gospels, but we must bring our heads as well. We must break through our fear to understand that these were *people* who were with Jesus, who formed a church, who wrote the Gospels—people like you and me. Understanding these people and their world, I hope, will free the Spirit more than ever in our lives.

There is every indication that fundamentalism is a growing phenomenon in our society. Fundamentalism refuses to listen to what the Gospel authors are really saying to their communities. It enters into a nonhistorical love affair with words—I don't know how else to describe it. The human need for clarity and certitude leads fundamentalists to use sacred writings in a mechanical, closed-ended, and authoritarian manner. This invariably leaves them trapped in their own cultural moment in history, and they often totally miss the real message, along with the deepest challenges and consolations of Scripture.

In the name of taking the word literally, the fundamentalist is, in fact, missing the literal word. Isn't that ironic? The real meaning of the text is largely missed by people who say they take it all literally. In other words, the metaphorical sense, the mythological sense, the sense of religious psychology and sacred story are, in fact, the literal, real sense—just as it is when you and I talk, write, and communicate with one another.

There is an especially telling passage in Mark's Gospel, where Jesus becomes angry even with his disciples, who are unable to understand his clearly metaphorical language. He tells them to watch out for the leaven of the Pharisees and the leaven of Herod. Taking him literally, they begin looking quizzically at one another because they do not have any bread (see Mark 8:14–16). Was Herod Bread a new brand that they had not heard about?

Aware of their amazing ability to miss the point, Jesus answers with impatience and a demand that they understand his language: "Do you think I am talking about bread? You're still not using your heads, are you? You still don't get the point, do you? Are you just dense? Though you have ears, you still don't hear. Though you have eyes, you still don't see!" (See Mark 8:17–19.)

Jesus knows the language necessary to speak of spiritual things and insists that his disciples learn it. Religion has always needed the language of metaphor, symbol, story, and analogy to point to the transcendent universe. There is actually no other way. Against conventional wisdom, such usage does not demand less of us, but much more. Maybe that is why we so consistently avoid sacred story in favor of mere mechanical readings that we can limit and control.

So, my goal in this book will be to delve into the language of religion and emerge with a clearer understanding of the Sermon on the Mount, the Nazarene rabbi who preached it, and the Gospel writers, especially Matthew, who passed it on to us. It may feel strange to approach Scripture this way, but, just as God spoke to the ancients in their moment in time, we trust that God will do the same for us. The Gospels thus lead us both to faith in the Jesus who lived in our history and to faith in the eternally risen Christ, who is still teaching and still hidden within his people.

The final and full word, therefore, is that the authority of the Bible lies not just in ancient texts but in the living Christ of history: church, community, and our own experience confirming its truth. The mystery is "Christ among you, your hope of glory" (Colossians 1:27)—this is the *living* Bible!

Finally, I must confirm and quote my mentor the Apostle Paul, who wrote a most strange but truthful thing. He stated, "Christ sent me not to baptize, but to preach the Gospel; and not by means of *wisdom* of language, wise words which would make the cross of Christ pointless" (1 Corinthians 1:17, emphasis mine). I know that I am not primarily a baptizer or a writer, although I do both, but a preacher. These written words may not be eloquent, but they are, I hope, new proclamation of the power and meaning of the cross for human history. If you perceive the message, I will know it was not because of a well-written text of mine, but because the cross has still not been emptied of its power to transform human history. That alone will last.

part one

Getting Ready to Hear Jesus

chapter one

Jesus' New World Order

I am told that there are three kinds of cultures today, each with their own "bottom line": political cultures based on the manipulation of power, economic cultures based on the manipulation of money, and religious cultures based on the manipulation of some theory about God. (The purely kinship-based cultures are largely disappearing.) These are the directions that human cultures take whenever they are left to their own devices. All three are based on some form of violence, although it is usually denied by most participants and hidden from the superficial observer. Evil gains its power from concealment, it seems. It is precisely this disguise and death that God, in Jesus, has come to destroy.

Jesus announced, lived, and inaugurated for history a new social order that is an actual alternative to each of the above—and an alternative that is inevitable not by reason of scientific determinism, but by the promise and grace of God. He called it the *Kingdom* or *Reign of God*. It is the subject of his inaugural address and the majority of his parables, and clearly the guiding image of his entire ministry. It was also the reason that he was killed: "It is better for one man to die for the people" (John 18:14) than to question the bottom line that is holding the whole system together.

When we Christians accept that Jesus was killed for the same reasons that people have been killed in all of human history (not because he walked around saying, "I am God"), we will have turned an important corner on our Jesus quest. He was rejected, as we will see, much more because of his worldview than his God-view. Yet we know that they are intrinsically connected. This now-and-not-yet Reign of God is the foundation for our personal hope and our cosmic optimism, but it is also the source of our deepest alienation from the world as it is. It will leave us as strangers and nomads on this earth (see Hebrews 11:13). Our task is to learn how to live in both worlds until they become one world—at least in us.

Once this guiding vision became clear to Jesus, which seems to have happened when he was about thirty and alone in the desert, everything else came into perspective. In fact, Matthew's Gospel states (4:17), "From then onward," Jesus began his preaching. He had his outer and absolute reference point that allowed him to judge and evaluate everything else properly. This was his Archimedean point, if you will, from which he could—and did—move the whole world.[1] His center point was clear and unquestionable—which is the precise nature of faith—and that allowed him to live and teach with the same simple clarity and certitude.

This center point, however, is not an idea or a theory about anything (which differentiates it from the other three kinds of culture), but, in fact, a Person—a thoroughly reliable and even lovable person that he calls his "Father." This new world order is based on the encounter with God who is experienced personally. Jesus seems to be saying that God is not a philosophical system, a theory to be proven, or an energy to be discussed or controlled, although we have often reduced God to such. Jesus believes that God is a Person to be imitated, enjoyed, and loved. We seem to know God only by relating to God, almost as if God refuses to be known apart from love. It is all about relationship. As Martin Buber (1878–1965), the Jewish philosopher mystic, put it, "All real living is meeting."[2] That simple and totally available experience makes all the difference in the world.

Jesus' new alternative is not just another religious culture, however. This is pivotal to understanding the unique character of his new world order.

As opposed to a religious culture, which is always using God for cultural purposes of control and manipulation through religious imagery, the Reign of God disallows both possibilities. This is the difference between true transcendence and its disguises, between the true sacred and what we might call the false sacred. The false sacred can be spotted because it is always self-serving and other destroying. Anthropologist Rene Girard (1923–2015) called it "the old sacrificial system," for it uses and misuses God to sacralize the creation of victims.[3] It might be "old," but, as we know, we continue this universal pattern to our own day, and in ever more sophisticated ways.

It seems to begin with Cain's killing of his brother, Abel, when Cain feels unworthy and unloved by Yahweh God. We know we are dealing with a universal and archetypal pattern that continues through time when even the very first chapters of the Bible tell us that brother kills brother. The "evil" one must always be killed so that "I" can be worthy, loved, and moral. Another group, nationality, class, or religion has to be named wrong so that "I" can feel right.

The insecure and false self seems to need an enemy to scapegoat so that it can feel superior and saved. False gods, by definition, must be appeased. The true God needs nothing. The true God invites us into an unthinkable communion.

Ironically, a religious culture actually works to a degree and for a time. It gives individuals and groups enough sense of cohesion and solidarity to create a partial community. With our immorality cleverly denied and carried by the scapegoated person or group, we actually feel rather good about ourselves. There was great American camaraderie for the twenty-some years following World War II. Our evil lay unrecognized on the heads of Germans, Japanese, and Communists. They were the bad losers, and we were the good victors. It was true on a certain political level, but not necessarily true at all on the level that Jesus says is final and definitive. It is no surprise that many people continue to confuse a merely religious culture (read: law and order) with the much more subversive Reign of God.

The true sacred, which is synonymous with the Reign of God, is of an entirely different order and significance. On the level of experience, the true sacred always reveals that:

God is One and for all.

God is sovereign to any group ownership or personal manipulation.

God is available as free gift and not through sacrificing another.

God needs no victims and creates no victims.

Jesus personifies this type of God and speaks defiantly in defense of such a God. Nowhere is he more succinct than when he quotes the Prophet Hosea, "Go and learn the meaning of the words: Mercy is what pleases me, not sacrifice" (Matthew 9:13).

Creating Idols

When there is no experience of the true sacred, we will always fall into the worship of the false sacred. The false sacred will invariably become a pretext and even a holy justification for prejudice, marginalization of others, scapegoating, and violence. If God is not God, in other words, we will ourselves become gods and create strange gods. Why wouldn't we? If God is not God, we will also demonize others as a way of validating our fragile identity. Such a pattern has become increasingly apparent in human history. Only an entrance into great compassion frees us from the need to divide our reality into the good guys and the bad guys, or, as Jesus puts it, "Be children of your Father in heaven, for he causes his sun to rise on the bad as well as the good, and sends down rain to fall on the upright and the wicked alike" (Matthew 5:44–45).

Without a forgiveness great enough to embrace even the obscure side of things, we are burdened (and I do mean *burdened*) with our own need to explain and to judge everything. Who is *right* now? Who was *wrong* there? These are eventual and important moral questions, but we cannot, we dare not, lead with them. If we do, we make love and compassion impossible. This is the centrality, and yet unbelievability, of Jesus' words, "Do not judge" (Matthew 7:1).

The true sacred, the Reign of God, unmasks and relativizes the false sacred. It is revolutionary in the truest sense of the term. The true sacred desacralizes all else and yet, ironically, establishes the basis for the authentic holiness of everything else. It is a paradox that the modern world resists. There is no real philosophical basis for calling something holy or sacred unless we are recognizing a transcendent origin, that which is beyond our creation and our control. Once the true sacred is honored, however, we are free and even compelled to recognize its reflection in all its creatures and all of creation. Thus, Jesus' name for God implies not only benevolence but also source and origin: Father. (Gender is not the emphasis, although one could say that defining healthy and true fatherhood had both the intention and the effect of subverting all patriarchy and false masculinity.)

Without the true sacred, we are all at one another's mercy and subject to one another's whimsical judgments. Under the true sacred, we are at the mercy of One Who Is Mercy. No wonder Jesus gave all his life to proclaim such a monumental liberation! Humanity has been waiting for such freedom with Messianic hope. It is the only way out of our revolving hall of mirrors, our own war of all against all, and is rightly called salvation. For Jesus, God's judgment is good news for the nations—and for the individual too. How different this is than how most of us think about judgment.

Conversion: Theme of the New World Order

Such a new world order is so foundationally different, so transformative of perspective, that mere education or intellectual assent is inadequate for even preliminary understanding. It demands what becomes Jesus' next favorite theme—conversion: a complete turnaround of worldviews. His teaching is summarized in one line: "The time is fulfilled, and the Reign of God is close at hand. Repent, and believe the Gospel" (Mark 1:15). Conversion is not a learning as much as it is an unlearning. Conversion is an unlearning that comes like a dove descending (see Mark 1:10) once the old world order is unmasked and the Great Lover is revealed. No wonder we had to use phrases like falling from a horse, scales falling from our eyes (see Acts 9:18), and the crowing of the cock (Luke 22:61).

We will not, of course, turn away from what seems like the only game in town (political, economic, or religious) unless we have glimpsed a more attractive alternative. Jesus is a living parable, an audiovisual icon of that more attractive alternative. We cannot even imagine it, much less imitate it, unless we see one human being do it first. Jesus has forever changed human imagination, and we are now both burdened and gladdened by the new possibility. There is good news to counter the deadening bad news, but we first have to be turned away from a conventional way of seeing.

The most unsettling aspect of his alternative wisdom, and perhaps the most consistent, is that the outcast is in the head-start position, precisely because he or she has been excluded from the false sacred system—the only game in town. Jesus thus begins with a most incredible statement: The poor are the blessed ones! (See Matthew 5:3.) Life has already freed them from the lie that the rest of us cannot see. They are potentially turned around and given a symbolic advantage in hearing the truth: "I tell you, tax collectors and prostitutes are making their way into the Reign of God before you" (Matthew 21:31). If the system is a mess, those outside of it are at a significant advantage.

Empathy for the victim, therefore, became the most subversive element in Jesus' teaching, although he was only building on his Jewish tradition and sympathies. This teaching was so hard to comprehend that he had to finally *image* it in the manner of his passion and death so we would get the message. As we see in the Gospels, Mark's in particular, the disciples themselves cannot get it. Most of the church is still in the early stages of comprehension. Why would the "first be last" (one of his most common one-liners) unless there is something essentially mistaken about the system in which we are all trying to be first, especially if we have tried really hard?

Against all odds, the one rejected by the norms of religion and culture, church and state, Jerusalem and Rome, the one crucified outside the walls became the Lord of history! In truth, his life and death have turned human wisdom and judgment upside down. Paul later refers to it as "the folly of the cross" and often waxes eloquently on this theme (for example, 1 Corinthians 1:17–31). Religious anthropologist Gil Bailie calls it "the gospel virus."[4] It is enough to infect and save the world from itself and for the truth.

Once the victim becomes Lord, we will have a healthy mistrust of all attempts at domination, exclusion, and victimization of others. If we were that wrong once about what is good and what is evil, we had best be suspicious about the claims of all righteous judgments. They might just be wrong again. Self-criticism is an outstanding characteristic of the Jewish tradition. They are one of the few peoples who incorporate into their sacred scriptures prophetic denunciations of *themselves*. This unusual capacity for critical thinking becomes a hallmark of Jesus' own relationship with his tradition, and, one could say, it becomes a unique characteristic of groups influenced by the Gospel. We call it the prophetic tradition. Without it, all groups and religions become idolatrous of themselves.

More positively, we are encouraged to welcome strangers, for by doing so, many people have entertained angels unaware (see Hebrews 13:2). As Jesus put it in his only description of the final judgment, "in so far as you did this to one of the least of these, you did it to me" (Matthew 25:40). I wonder what else could save us from our fear and accusation of one another, except one whose judgments are both upside-down and true—and whose mercy is everlasting. Fortunately, they are one and the same, a God who is both sanctuary and stumbling stone (see Isaiah 8:14).

We Need More and More of What Doesn't Work

It seems that only contact with the true sacred will effectively inoculate us from the many forms of the false sacred. In the converse of the first commandment, we might say, "If you do not worship the Lord as God, you will have strange gods before you." We might call the strange gods celebrities, jobs, self-image, security, money, family, or power, but we honor and worship them with the same fervor that the saints reserved for God. It is amazing that folks do not see this.

Strange gods would be easy to recognize and dethrone if they were obviously evil, ugly stone statues, or the pagan gods of religions other than our own. But the substitutes for the true sacred are probably as well-denied and disguised today as they were in Jesus' time. The obvious idols are money, sex, and power. The less obvious idols are even more devious, precisely because they are usually partial reflections of the true sacred. They give us just enough transcendence to sometimes inoculate us from the further journey toward their source. This is especially true in the lives of good, well-educated, and well-intentioned people. One of the ironies of the Gospel is that it is the well-bred people who fight Jesus the most. Let's look at some of our blockages.

Anything mysterious or unknown often feels spiritual, and people will speak of it in hushed tones as holy or sacred. Similarly, things that are secret, silent, or hidden often have a numinous quality for many people. Consider how a good science fiction movie often inspires awe in its viewers.

That which is famous, well-known, or publicly observed has a larger-than-life quality for many people. In the absence of any real sacred stories, media events like public scandals, dramas, and rock star activities take on a more-than-deserved quality. We could say that these have become the daily fuel of many people's entire lives. Cheap gas can keep a car going, but it eventually destroys the engine.

For some reason, that which is huge, large, or powerful inspires awe and wonder in many people. Stand at the bottom of a solid rock canyon and you will somehow hear ancient voices and eternal meanings. Watch little boys' eyes when they see a strong man in action or young girls' eyes when they watch a beautifully dressed bride walk down the aisle. These are clearly images of gods and goddesses.

The natural, the wildness and freedom of nature, transforms many people. All their lives, they long to return, as if nothing else is real in comparison. Are they perhaps right? The Franciscan tradition has always seen all creation as the footprints and fingerprints of God and therefore sacramental. This is true of many native spiritualities and Christian creation spirituality too. It is much needed today if we are to rediscover the integrity of creation and prevent its wholesale destruction through climate change.

Anything that is old, ancestral, or traditional ties us up with the timeless and the eternal. Listen to people's voices as they enter old ruins or uncover a piece of family history. They sigh.

The truly beautiful, the magnificent, the poetic all feel like ends in themselves—enough to satisfy. Joy and pleasure are surely promises and enticements, free samples that tell us we are on track toward the same.

Surely God makes use of all these initial experiences of the holy. Yet philosophically there is no real ground for calling them sacred or holy. They are reflectors of light, but not the source of light itself. This absolute and ultimate God-centeredness, this demand for the true sacred, is at the heart of Jesus' teaching. His new world order rises and falls on this diamond edge, and it seems to be enough if only a few are convinced of it. Merely a "leaven" of true believers in the true sacred is all that is needed to raise the whole loaf (see Matthew 13:33).

We Need a Yardstick

Unless we are confronted by true otherness, we will spend our lives rattling around inside our own world of preferences without any criteria to evaluate or critique them. There is no north star to guide our little ship, lost in a sea of time. True transcendence, the Reign of God, becomes the measure by which all cultures and human actions are to be judged: "You yourselves will sit on twelve thrones to judge the twelve tribes of Israel" (Matthew 19:28). This absence is the weakness and the continuing chaos of modern multiculturalism. Whose values prevail? By what criteria is this culture superior and that culture inferior? Are the measuring lines economic, political, aesthetic, or familial? Although the world has suffered much from the various forms of Christian colonialism, the world has nothing to fear from either the message or the methods of the true Jesus. We are all winners in the Reign of God.

Jesus is teaching that *right relationship* is the ultimate and daily criterion. If a social order allows and encourages, and even mandates, good connectedness between people and creation, people and events, people and people, and people and God, then we have a truly sacred culture: the Reign of God. The world as it would be if God were directly in charge would be a world of right relationship. It would not be a world without pain or mystery, but simply a world where we would be in good contact with all things, where we would be connected and in communion. Conversely, the work of the Evil One is always to separate, divide, and throw apart (*dia-bolical*).

Right relationship is all about union and communion, it seems, which means that it is also about forgiveness, letting go, service, and lives of patience and simplicity. Who can doubt that this is the sum and substance of Jesus' teaching? He makes right relationship desirable, possible, and the philosopher's stone by which everything else is to be weighed and judged.

In the Reign of God, the very motive for rivalry, greed, and violence has been destroyed. Philosophically, we can see that the historical Jesus is the formal cause for the destruction of death. (A formal cause gives shape, image, and direction to a final effect.) Anthropologically, we can say that history and cultures have been slowly but definitely directed away from their justifications for violence and their rationalizations for greed by the life and teaching of Jesus. Psychologically, our death wishes are transmuted into a calming hope that feels like life-written-large. Scripturally, "He went up to the heights, took captives" (Ephesians 4:8). Spiritually, he unmasks our love affair with death by teaching us to recognize it as death and to weep over it. In those tears over the pain of Jesus and the pain of the world, we discover the lie, and, in the same moment, the compassion that absorbs it. We cannot get much better than that.

Probably the imagery of Jesus as scapegoat is one of the more undeveloped themes in Christian Scriptures studies. Recent investigations of the Mishnah and other extra-biblical sources have helped us make a series of connections that were probably natural for first-century Judaism: The striking with the reed, the spitting on the scapegoat, the crowning, the entanglement with thorns, and the scarlet cloak were all ways that the scapegoat was treated before being sent out into the desert. These rituals all developed from the original one mandated in Leviticus 16:7–10, 21–22. Perhaps we needed to see how universal and basic the scapegoating mechanism is for human culture before we could see the importance of Jesus' replacement of it. The passion accounts in the Gospels have little impact beyond that we should feel sad—unless we see Jesus as a cosmic archetype and answer. He is truly Job, Jeremiah, the sign of Jonah, and the Suffering Servant of Isaiah, all in one. Jesus is everyman and everywoman. Jesus is the human dilemma—answered.

The Freedom That Sets Us Free

Crucial to Jesus' new world order are some very special understandings of freedom that must be clarified for the modern and postmodern mind. Without God's definition of freedom, we will continue to use the Gospel as if it were a product that can be bought, sold, imposed, or attained. The Gospel is not a competing ideology that is threatened by anything outside its pale. It is not one of the so-called ten thousand things, but the Gospel is that by which we compare and evaluate the ten thousand things. It is the light of the world that illuminates the whole household (see Matthew 5:14); it is the yeast and not the whole loaf (see Matthew 13:33); it is the salt that gives flavor and nutrition to the much larger meal (see Matthew 5:13).

Once we can accept that Jesus has given us an illuminating lens by which to see and measure all things, we can no longer treat Christianity as a threat, nor allow it to be a threat, to human or cultural freedom. It is, in fact, true freedom's greatest ally, as will become clearer. The Gospel is a process much more than a product, a style more than a structure, a person more than a production. It is a way of being in the world that will always feel like compassion, mercy, and spaciousness—at least to honest and healthy people.

The Gospel threatens nothing but death and *equally* critiques every culture. It is identical with no culture or institution, even the church. As John's Gospel states so poetically, the Spirit blows where it will (see 3:8). How different and healing Western history could have been if we had received such Gospel freedom and modeled it for others.

Jesus has not come to impose Christendom like an imperial system. The evidence for such later attempts is absolutely nil in the teaching of Jesus. In fact, he consistently warns against it. Wherever we have tried it, the long-term results have been disastrous: countries of baptized pagans or merely religious cultures that thought they were the Reign of God.

The Gospel flourishes in the realm of true freedom. I do not think that Jesus ever expected that the whole world would become formally Christian, but I do believe that his truth about right relationship, his proclamation of the power of powerlessness, is the message that will save the world from self-destruction and for an eternal truth. I do believe that Jesus is therefore rightly called the Savior of the World and is able to do it through a minority position. Jesus enters the imperial city on a donkey. He is the turning point of history.

Multiculturalism, which is the world's only possible future, has nothing to fear and a great deal to learn from the wisdom of the Gospel. Unfortunately, it is going to take a few centuries to reconvince most of the world because of our past track record of economic, political, and spiritual colonialism. The Gospel will always insist that means and ends must be in complete agreement, or the final end is always polluted. There is no way to peace; peace is the way. There is no path toward love except by practicing love. War will always produce more war. Violence can never bring about true peace.

Much of the content of the Sermon on the Mount has to do with this agreement between means and ends. (It is one of the most ignored aspects of Jesus' teaching, and I am convinced it explains the attraction of many former Christians to Buddhism and nonviolent teaching. They had to leave home to find out what was hidden in their own histories.)

Furthermore, Jesus has a different understanding of personal freedom too. Freedom is not the capacity to be what we are not, but the capacity to be fully who we already are, to develop our inherent selves as much as God allows. The perfect and full freedom of a fig tree is to become a perfect and full fig tree. Thus, Jesus curses one that does not (see Matthew 21:19). Contrary to our Western understanding since the French Revolution and the Enlightenment, it is not freedom for a fig tree to try to bear oranges or apples, or to try to be a horse or a wastebasket. Surely there is a certain freedom from constraint here, but this is not a very helpful kind of freedom. It only frustrates and finally destroys. It obstructs the fig tree's own fruitfulness and makes its own success impossible. It cannot work.

Many of us are like sick or dead fig trees, but with happy faces painted on our anemic apples, shouting, "But I'm free!" Our addictive society has to do what it wants to do. The freedom offered by all great spiritual traditions is quite different. Spiritual and true freedom is wanting to do what we have to do to become who we are. For some reason, humans rebel at what feels like an external mandate. When we listen for a while, we can often realize that it is also our deepest inner desire. The truth that all things desire to be themselves now has a different ring to it! No longer is it a scary search for private authenticity, but a patient acceptance of truth. Such is the difference between wisdom and mere reaction, and it takes most of us awhile to get there.

We will not appreciate Jesus' loyalty to the Law and the Prophets if we do not accept his deeper understanding of freedom. I'm afraid that the cry of the French Revolution, "Liberty, equality, and fraternity," has formed us much more than the Jesus Revolution. His cry might instead be "Identity, justice, and community." Think about the difference.

We also tend to think of freedom as freedom of movement and the liberty to choose between options. This is surely a good and important freedom. There is no indication that the great spiritual teachers, Jesus included, see it as essential, however. They seem to recognize that the world of preferences and possibilities does not of itself lead to wisdom, truth, or even depth of experience. In fact, in the spiritual life, the rule seems to be that less is more. There is almost no correlation between the number of options and the amount of truth or goodness that one attains.

The saints usually seek to under-stimulate themselves, lessen their options, choose lives of poverty, and flourish quite well in situations of imprisonment, persecution, and opposition. Our notion of freedom as options and movement is a pleasant luxury, but not what Jesus is seeking when he goes into the desert; when he seems to limit himself in terms of family, marriage, and a place to "lay his head"; or when he even accepts the limitations of a short ministry among uneducated people at a low period of religion in a country occupied by a foreign oppressor. That's not much freedom by *our* definition, but more than enough for him to say, "the Reign of God is among you" (Luke 17:21).

Apocalypse Now

It is commonly said that Jesus, and most of the Christian Scriptures authors, believed that the end of the world was right around the corner. Many passages in Paul's letters and the Gospels would lead us to believe that this was their expectation. It *was*, but not in the way we think. It would be much closer to the truth to say that because the old order of the world (cultures built on money, power, and mere religiosity) had now been so clearly exposed and defeated by the Jesus event, they thought it was only a matter of time until everybody would see through it all! I do suppose that both Jesus and Paul are still more than a little disappointed that it has taken so long to defeat the lie. I guess they were optimists about our capacity and desire for great truth.

"It's all over" can be understood in two very different ways: either it is all going to hell, or it is all becoming heaven. In either case, we stop taking the status quo as the final state of affairs. The burden of much modern thinking, which often leads to nihilism, is that it believes neither one. It gives the system too much credence on either the liberal or the conservative side. It has to fix and figure it all out by itself and through the latest research. No wonder it leads to nihilistic disbelief in anything. The daily evidence surely seems to be pointing to the first: It is all going to hell. The promise of God and the raising up of Jesus point, however, to the second: It is still becoming heaven, so do not give up and even do what you can to live the final reality now—and despite the evidence. We call it faith.

The apocalyptic readings that we come across in the Gospels (Matthew 24, Mark 13, and Luke 21:5–33) are not doomsday at all—unless our bottom line is wrong! They free us from propping up what is falling apart anyway. They keep us from wasting time on passing images. They keep us from putting our eggs into baskets with big holes in the bottom. They are not addressing the end of the world as much as the falling apart of worlds. Without such a clarifying and honest evaluation, we would live in a very incoherent world, an absurd and frightful world of constant loss and destruction of the very things that we thought were essential and even good. Now we know what to expect, what is worth rejoicing in, and where to place our bets. Loss and death are part of the process.

Jesus' teaching is that this new world order has already begun, and he clearly seems to see himself as its herald, its inauguration, and its personal assurance. No wonder he is forever central for us. He is the game plan in microcosmic form, but with one added difficulty: What is *now* in him is both *now and not yet* in us. Here is the source of almost all our problems with faith, trials, and opposition. We must look at this closely.

Living in Between

All great religions advise a certain degree of necessary opposition, a refining of the question, a deep choosing of our true position that comes only through time and trial. Some Native religions say that human life must be lived on the edge of a knife. It must not be so comfortable that we lose contact with the struggle, and yet there must be enough security to sustain us through the trials. The promise of the Reign of God does not offer us pie in the sky, but just enough finger food to keep us nibbling and hoping for more: the now. The promise of the Reign of God does not take away the opposition, but, in fact, ensures it: the not yet. That is the razor's edge of full-faith existence. We must stay on the knife.

The old world order, however, is trying to create a society where we do not have to live on the edge of the knife. An economic culture is trying to eliminate as much inconvenience and discomfort as possible. It encourages increase in one tiny area—money—as the answer to all other areas. This most fragile premise takes much more faith to believe than the holistic truth of the Gospel, yet most of the world seems to believe it. It promises to give us a relaxed and tension-free life, off that razor's edge. If it worked, I could see why people would buy it. But we need more and more of what does not work. This addiction is clearly the nature of economic cultures.

A political culture tries to eliminate all opposition and obstacle, as if life were attained by obliterating enemies and differences. Even the church often descends to this pagan level, as Jesus calls it (see Matthew 20:25), when it resorts to dominative power and even punitive means to enforce its will. At that point, prayerful people know that there is little real trust in the presence of the Risen Jesus in history. He never relied upon enforcement in his lifetime; I do not know why he would change his strategy now. There is a soul knowledge, a victory of the Spirit, that comes only from engagement, patience, prayer, insight, and inner transformation. It is never attained by mere political victories or control of outcomes. In fact, when a Christian needs to ensure outcomes, we know they are outside the realm of faith. When we do not need to control the future, we are in a very creative and liminal space where God is most free to act in our lives. Faith seems to be the attitude that Jesus most praises in people, maybe because it makes hope and love possible.

There is no such thing as a victory of the Spirit if it is attained by coercion, mere mandate, or social pressure. Paul said it in great urgency and anger to his community at Galatia: "Are you foolish enough to resort to the law for what you began in the Spirit? Has grace been wasted on you? If this is so, it most certainly has been wasted" (see 3:3). Wow! How did that become lost in the Tradition? A political culture, like the Russian Federation, will always use power in totalitarian ways to achieve its purposes. We can never expect Caesar to do Christ's work. We can never proclaim the exodus from Pharaoh's palace. If we try, as we surely have, it will always be on the ruler's terms. You would think we would know that by now.

A religious culture is one that is trapped in such a confusion. It mixes up belief in God with cultural order and institutional stability. It needs and wants a great policeman in the sky to keep everything in line. I can surely understand the need, especially when it works rather efficiently and does keep people at some early stages of needed morality. A religious culture has much to recommend it, sort of like John the Baptist in his early stages. He baptized in water, enforced some needed moralities, and, according to Jesus, neither ate nor drank (see Matthew 11:18). He was a good and religious man, as far as that goes, yet Jesus makes a most amazing statement that we have usually glossed over: "[Of] all the children born to women, there has never been anyone greater than John the Baptist; yet the least in the Reign of Heaven is greater than he" (Matthew 11:11).

Perhaps a religious culture, symbolized very well by John the Baptist, is the most common precursor for the full Reign of God, symbolized by Jesus. I personally believe that is the usual pattern. Religion is the best, and it is the worst (for the corruption or misuse of the best is the worst). We need religious cultures that are not afraid to speak of God, but we do not need religious cultures that use and misquote God for their own purposes or become ends in themselves. Like John the Baptist, they must be ready to become smaller so Christ can become larger (see John 3:30). Such cases of institutional or national forgetfulness are rather rare, I am afraid. Some would insist that the very nature of institutions is to perpetuate and protect themselves, even church institutions.

The Reign of God never sells humanity short. In Paul's later description, he forbids us to trivialize God's plan: "A privilege of yours must not be allowed to give rise to harmful talk; for it is not eating and drinking that make the Reign of God, but the saving justice, the peace and joy brought by the Holy Spirit" (Romans 14:16–17). There is a certain challenge that is proper to, and needed by, human nature. We seem to need some obstacles that are worthy of our energy and passion. The soul is not slovenly and flourishes only in the presence of a certain opposition. As Simone Weil (1909–1943) put it, truth and affliction are necessary allies.[5] When Jesus offers the great repayment for loss of house, brothers, sisters, father, children, and land (see Mark 10:30), he adds only one extra reward to the promise of a hundredfold return—and that is persecution! That doesn't sound like a reward—unless communion and love are the final goals.

There Is Only the Supernatural

Near the end of the Hebrew Scriptures, the prophet Zechariah says that when God's day comes, there will be no distinction between sacred and profane, temple and marketplace: Even the horse bells will be inscribed with the word "sacred," and in the Temple of Yahweh the very cooking pots will be as fine as the sprinkling bowls at the altar (see 14:20). The Reign of God is not about churchiness at all. It has everything to do with everything. In fact, as we read Jesus' images and examples, it appears that it is in the world of house and field, job and marriage where we are converted to right relationship.

The secular has become the place where we encounter the true sacred. As Catholic theology would proclaim, it is a sacramental universe. It is the domestic church that converts us; it is the job of the liturgical church to send us back there. It is the unexciting world of details, diapers, and women who have lost one dime (see Luke 15:8–10) that appears to offer the teachable moment for Jesus. It is much more important, it seems, than the world of stipends, sermons, and sacristies, which tend to become their own industry.

An Upside-Down World

There is a telling phrase that is used in the Acts of the Apostles to describe this new sect that is upsetting the old world order in Thessalonica. The Christians of that town were dragged before the city council and called "the people who have been turning the whole world upside down...they have broken Caesar's edicts" (Acts 17:6–7). People are not called before the city council for mere inner beliefs or new attitudes unless they are also upsetting the social order. We will see that the import of Jesus' teaching and almost all of his healing and nature miracles was a rearranging of social relationships and therefore of social order. Someone does not go around eating with the underclass, touching the untouchables, sending lepers back into polite society as a testimony (see Mark 1:44), and collaborating with upstarts down at the river without turning traditional societies upside down. City councils are not places that we go for profound wisdom; their job is to hold societies together where they are always held together—at the level of conventional wisdom: "the way we always do it here in Thessalonica." One of the major weaknesses of the Christian understanding of Jesus is that we really do not understand what it was that made Jesus worth killing. It was not because he walked around saying, "I am God."

There are four principal areas of conventional wisdom that Jesus seems to ignore, oppose, or even subvert: family, possessions, status, and the very nature of sacrificial religion. We will see that these were enough to get him killed. We will be looking for this alternative wisdom of Jesus in the rest of this book.

chapter two

Not Business as Usual

He was still speaking to the crowds when suddenly his mother and his brothers were standing outside and were anxious to have a word with him. But to the man who told him this, Jesus replied, "Who is my mother? Who are my brothers?" And stretching out his hand toward his disciples, he said, "Here are my mother and my brothers. Anyone who does the will of my Father in heaven is my brother and sister and mother." (Matthew 12:46–50)

To challenge family was really shocking to a culture based on the kinship system. In fact, a pivotal point in Matthew's Gospel, the symbolic middle of the Gospel, is this scene where Jesus creates a new definition of family.

Jesus switches sides. He's on the inside of a house teaching his disciples when his mother shows up. Mary is standing *outside* with "his brothers" and the word is sent to Jesus, *inside*, that his mother and brothers want to see him. And he says, "Who is my mother? Who are my brothers?" Then he points to his disciples and says, "Here are my mother and my brothers. Anyone who does the will of my Father in heaven is my brother and sister and mother" (Matthew 12:48–50; see also Mark 3:31–35).

Jesus has, in a moment, turned upside down the whole bloodline family system, even at the risk of slighting his mother! That's utterly shocking and unacceptable to his culture. Jesus says it's not blood that makes family;

it's trust, union, and commitment. He has redefined family in a kinship-based culture (which is often the shape of religious cultures). From that point, after Matthew 12, everything turns to those outside—who are, of course, invited *inside* (where Mary and Jesus' "brothers" surely are).

The scene is presented as a scandalous passage so we can't miss the point: How could he dare to consider his own mother an outsider? Well, he is willing for us to think that so we will redefine what family is. Jesus opposes conventional wisdom so much that he has redefined the family in terms of the universal family of love. Looking back over two thousand years, how many wars have been justified by kinship? Yet Jesus broke that addiction to false patriotism, loyalty, and nationality.

Jesus also questioned conventional wisdom regarding wealth and possessions. That should be obvious, but it hasn't been at all. The church itself, which was supposed to be a new social ethic, became very comfortable with wealth and possessions after Constantine made it the state religion in the year 313. We moved from underground catacombs to princely basilicas.

I realize what Saints Dominic (1170–1221) and Francis (1181–1226) were trying to do by creating a new kind of clergy who would take a vow of poverty and not be a part of the ruling class or wealth system. The initials we Franciscans put after our names are OFM, which stand for Order of Friars Minor. In modern language, it would be "brothers of the lower class." Mendicants—beggars—are, by definition, outside the production/consumption economy.

Francis switched sides from the upper class to the lower class because he knew that only from the side of powerlessness could one be entrusted with the Gospel. Those who stay on the side of power have consistently misused and misinterpreted the Gospel. Francis was a sociological genius without knowing it, especially in understanding how the Gospel could be heard, how the Gospel had to be preached and understood. In subsequent centuries, every religious order saw that. They all took the vow of poverty as an *essential* part of the Gospel life. The vow clearly was a choice, by a community and by each individual, to opt out of the economic system. Unfortunately, our communities eventually became corporately wealthy and now we have our stock portfolios. Isn't that a shame? Take the vow of poverty to opt out of the system, and then be sucked back into it!

The third area in which Jesus assaults conventional wisdom is social and religious recognition, the whole honor/shame system. He refuses to abide by it. He refuses to live up to what is considered honorable and refuses to shame what people consider shameful. (If that is not apparent in your reading of the Gospels, read them again.) This does not gain him many friends. It's perhaps the thing that most bothers the priests and the elders. In response to his ignoring the debt codes and purity codes, they decided to kill him (see Mark 3:6, 11:18; Matthew 12:14; Luke 19:47; and John 11:53). Even his family thought he was crazy (see Mark 3:21)!

Every culture and church has such an honor/shame system—even libertines who think they don't.

The New World Order

Chapter One discussed a new religious culture, but Jesus' vision has political implications too. When Jesus talked about the Reign of God, he was talking about an utterly different way of relating with one another than human society as we know it.

For example, the decades following World War II established a world order that has influenced us for most of our adult lives. It was the Cold War alignment, conveniently blessed by our theological understandings: We in the West were the good guys and the Communists were the bad guys.

We chose this understanding because the ego always wants to feel superior. The high moral ground the West took in the Cold War—along with our nuclear weapons—gave us a false sense of security. That all ended in

1991 with the collapse of the Soviet Union. Our Western leaders were suddenly scrambling to define a "new world order," in the words of former President George H. W. Bush (1924–2018). And they looked again to terms of power for ways to define themselves and their countries. I doubt very much that any major political leader would align a new world order in terms of cooperation, trust, service, and redemptive suffering!

My point is this: For all the talk of a new world order, it's simply the old world order. The politicians had no right to steal that phrase, especially when there is nothing *new* about it! The new world order—the Reign of God—is the heart of the Christian Scriptures, and it's a phrase to be taken seriously. Yet we have failed to understand the coming of Jesus as the dawn of a new age. For most Christians, life in the new age has been business as usual.

What is the new age Jesus talks about? In Matthew 19:23–26, Jesus describes the danger of riches. Peter then speaks up. "What about us?" he asks. "We have left everything and followed you. What are we to have, then?" (See Matthew 19:27.) It's an anxious question, because Jesus has just told them that anyone who leaves everything is going to do OK. "Jesus said to them, 'In truth I tell you, *when everything is made new again...*'" (Matthew 19:28a, emphasis added). He just assumes that things can be and will be constructed differently. Such a vision seems to be his starting point—even more than his practical goal. We have to share the *dream of God* before we know how to live and where to look for the truth.

"When all is made new," in the original Greek phrase, includes the word *palingenesia*—a unique word. It's rendered literally as "regeneration, a new genesis, an utterly new beginning," or, perhaps best, "a totally new birth in a totally new world." It's the only time the word is used in the Gospels.

The Acts of the Apostles will use another Greek phrase, *apocatastasis*, translated in *The Jerusalem Bible* as "universal restoration." That's in Peter's first sermon, and he's grown a bit since Matthew's Gospel. Now he courageously preaches that God "will send you the Christ God has predestined, that is Jesus, whom heaven must keep till the universal restoration comes which God proclaimed, speaking through the holy prophets" (Acts 3:20–21). In later theological language, this term was used to describe the restoration of all creation at the end, the reconciliation of all things in Christ (see Colossians 1:20). What a hopeful and positive apocalypse that would be! I personally love to believe that is the real meaning of the victory of Christ and the final resurrection.

What we will discover in the Christian Scriptures text, especially in Matthew's Gospel, is this new world order, a new age, a promised hope. This new age was not something the early Christians first understood as happening at the end of history; rather, it was ushered in by the teaching of Jesus. *Jesus was undercutting the system of human society, refusing to take it seriously—while continuing to love and serve it.*

Scripture scholar John P. Meier, referencing the Sermon on the Mount, writes that Jesus "was not proclaiming the reform of the world; he was proclaiming the end of the world."[6] And that's the point of this book: Jesus is not presenting a new program for human society. Jesus refuses to accept society on its own terms; he refuses to offer it allegiance as it is. When we read all the apocalyptic announcements of Jesus, how everything is going to fall apart, how the sun will fall from the heavens, we're reading that the world *as we know it* must and will end. We read here not so much of a final end of history, but an end to our own personally constructed worlds.

That's an experience that must first happen spiritually. It must happen in our psyche, in our relationships, and in our culture. One day it just happens. It's the moment of conversion, when, all of a sudden, we realize—not just in our head but also in our gut—that everything in this world is passing away. All is impermanent, socially constructed, and, in that sense, illusory.

The sad thing for many of us is that it doesn't happen until we confront death, usually the death of a loved one. In my own life, I became aware of the mortality of two friends with cancer, and, as I heard the sad news, I fell behind a haze: "It's all passing away. Nothing lasts," I thought. When we're young, it's very hard to believe that. It dawns on us the older we get and the more we experience death, failure, and what the Christian Scriptures call the cross.

But Jesus is not talking just about the death of friends. He means that the whole Gospel can't really be heard until we recognize the final, utter truth of this world. It's not a morbid recognition, but it is nonetheless an acceptance that everything except God is relative and is passing away. Any economic system that our government offers us is OK, but don't put too much trust in it: It's not any final answer. We can eat all the tofu we want and we will still die. All the guns in America will not give us the security of God.

Whether we vote for Democrats, Republicans, or Independents, we can't think that any of them can usher in the Reign of God. If we think, "Who could be that naïve?" don't forget that Americans have come very close to that kind of naïveté for most of our history.

Americans, like few other peoples, have known two hundred years of massive cultural idolatry. We think that our country, our form of government, our way of doing things fell straight from heaven, as if it were God's plan for the world. We think that if everyone would live like Americans, the world would be happy. Maybe people don't say it that way, but I know, as a preacher, the shock on people's faces when I dare to question it. That tells me they believe it. It is a cultural myth, which means it is unquestioned. It's a way of thinking, written between the lines and in the margins.

Idols, like cultural myths, are always disguised, if not totally invisible to the worshiper. If we could see their falsity, we would, of course, know that they are not God. So false gods, idols, must always dress up as a cultural virtue like success, love of country, or hard work. These loyalties, either hidden or expressed, must be exposed for the gods that they are. Until this happens, there will be nothing really *new* and God's dream cannot show itself.

Finally, what is most amazing, and therefore most overlooked by most Christians, is how much of Jesus' teaching is concerned with subverting conventional understandings of religion. It is, in fact, such a total critique of almost all early stage religion that it would be easy to view Jesus as antireligious. His anti-Temple shenanigans are, in fact, where he seems to cross the line. The Gospel text has him intentionally heading toward Jerusalem, where he has no doubt "the elders and the chief priests and the scribes" (Mark 8:31) will reject and seek to kill him. His good-boy disciples refuse to believe it, and miss the point, change the subject, or actively oppose him every time he brings it up (see Mark 8:31–10:45). Only an unnamed woman, clearly outside the circles of religious power, sees the handwriting on the wall. She knows what he is doing and where it will lead: "She has done what she could: She has anointed my body beforehand for its burial" (Mark 14:8).

He is living in a religious culture, which is finally what gets him killed. The bottom line here is God-talk that legitimizes an in-group and increasingly marginalizes more and more "unacceptable" people. The outcasts have to leave the Temple and go out to the river Jordan for the forgiveness of sin. For Jesus to join in John's baptism at that location outside of town was a symbolic critique of the whole Temple organization and its lend-lease brokerage system. For a religion that had clear controls on how sin could be forgiven, we have John pouring out forgiveness like free river water. No wonder the scribes and Pharisees came out to observe and threaten (see John 1:24–25). Their monopoly on God was being ignored by an announcement of living and ever-available water, from the very river that symbolized deliverance and freedom (see Joshua 3:10–17).

Subverting the Old World Order

Jesus' new world order is utterly subverting the old world order. This is what makes people so furious: Jesus simply ignores the systems of values and righteousness that are so important to them. That is much more subversive than it might seem on the surface. For example, by Jesus' reckoning, why would anyone try to become rich? It doesn't make a bit of sense once we know the really real. His approach is much more effective than mere fire-and-brimstone sermons on the evil of riches.

That experience of the really Real—the Reign of God experience—is the heart of Jesus' teaching. It's Reality with a capital R, the very bottom line, the pattern that connects. It's the goal of all true religion, the experience of the Absolute, the Eternal, what is. The Reign of God is Jesus' way of describing God's dream for the world.

Jesus talked about this dream constantly. In Matthew 9:17, Jesus says, "Nor do people put new wine into old wineskins; otherwise, the skins burst, the wine runs out, and the skins are lost. No; they put new wine into fresh skins and both are preserved." That's a very commonsense image for Jesus' agrarian peasant audience. Such colorful, real images—symbolic talk—communicate instantly.

Jesus' image is this: "I'm going to give you a new vision of the world that you will taste like new wine, but it isn't going to make a bit of difference unless you have some new wineskins. If there are not new structures that reflect the new attitude, then even the attitude will be lost. *Both* container and contents must be renewed—or they will both be lost."

We have traditionally tried to preach a Gospel largely of words, attitudes, and inner salvation experiences. People say they are saved, they're "born again," yet how do we really know if someone is saved? Do they love the poor? Are they free from their egos? Are they patient in the face of persecution? Those might be real indicators.

A so-called new attitude inside an old world order that we accept uncritically will finally dilute and even destroy the attitude. It's not enough to talk about some kind of new, inebriating wine, some new wisdom, without new wineskins, new structures, a new world order to support it. As Dorothy Day (1897–1980) is reputed to have said in her perfect Reign of God style, nothing is going to change until we stop accepting "this filthy, rotten system!"[7] That's not to say that people who are not of good-will, or are not journeying, will not be saved by that God. God will save them. But we need to be honest about the impact—or lack of impact—of the Gospel on Western civilization, on the world. That which has become standard and normative must first be called into serious question.

I have preached occasionally in Europe, in the so-called Christian nations that gave us what we thought was the Gospel. It's not a very pretty picture: Largely empty cathedrals are filled with golden angels and rococo statues. They have the outer structure, but there's no community inside the structure. More and more of the churches are empty, especially of men and the young.

One can make a strong case for the Christian nations being the most militaristic on earth—the greediest, the most untrue to the teacher they claim to follow. That's not to say our ancestors didn't have faith, or that Grandma and Grandpa were not good people. But, by and large, we did not produce a Christian *culture*. We produced some wonderfully liberated saints and Christian individuals. They tried to create some new wineskins, but often the church itself resisted their calls for any structural reform. Take even the father of my religious community, Saint Francis—he wasn't even dead yet when we moved him out of leadership and exiled him because we were afraid to take him seriously!

Assisi is another good example. Both the Rule and the Testament of Saint Francis tell us: Don't ever own or build your own buildings. At best, seek little churches where you can stay "as pilgrims and strangers." But have you been to Assisi? Poor Francis and Clare were so hated by the establishment of their time that they moved outside the walls of Assisi.

Now there's a giant church on one end of town where Francis is buried and on the other end of town a giant church where Clare is buried. Talk about divine irony! The town has been living off them for eight hundred years. They're selling little Francis and Clare dolls, but do they really do what Francis and Clare did? Probably not.

That's not to single out Assisi; we're all the same. It's easier to talk about the wine without the wineskins, to talk about salvation theories without any new world order. In honesty, the European nations that call themselves Christian base their society, as we all do, entirely upon structures of domination and control: racism, sexism, class, power, and money. They're built on all the things Jesus told us not to build on. That's a little bit of new wine in some very old wineskins.

It might be a little cynical, but you could almost figure out what Jesus said by looking at our history and naming the opposite of what we did. We keep worshiping the messenger, keeping Jesus up on statues and images, so we can avoid what Jesus said. It's the best smokescreen in the world! We just keep saying, "We love Jesus." The more we talk about Jesus, the less we'll do what he said. That's the way the ego fools itself—and, in this case, it's the way culture, nations, and even the churches have fooled themselves.

The Symbolism of the Temple and the End of Worlds

Jesus' sayings about the end of the world are a key to understanding his radical message. But before looking at these passages, it's important to address images and sacred mythology. Part of the reason why we've become so confused by the Scriptures is that we no longer understand sacred mythology. Modern popular understanding of mythology took a big jump with the PBS interviews by Bill Moyers of Joseph Campbell (1904–1987). Campbell, who fought Catholicism all his life, also admitted that it gave him his fascination with images. He bitterly regretted the liturgical changes of Vatican II. And, although his vision of Catholicism was severely limited, he had a point: We used to draw upon an immense treasure house of right-brain, nonrational, translucent images. We used incense a lot more, for example, with its intense aroma and mystifying visual presence. We had music—Gregorian chant—that hauntingly emphasized the otherworldly aspects of life. We've lost that to some degree during the past half-century and more. Though we wouldn't want to turn back many other things, our loss of right-brain liturgical action is a great loss to an entire generation of youth and overzealous reformers.

Images are very powerful and essential to religion. As the ground-breaking Swiss psychiatrist Carl Jung (1875–1961) stated, transformation takes place only in the presence of images, not concepts. Until we reimagine our God, ourselves, or our world, nothing ever happens. People born before the rational scientific revolution of the last few hundred years knew how to read sacred literature. They knew that time-tested mythology is always true and that the truth is conveyed in the symbols and stories themselves.

We moderns, tainted by the scientific method, have forgotten how to read sacred literature. We look for empirical truth when the stories are full of mythical, symbolic images. In order to understand our Scriptures, we must be willing to look for the symbols, to *treat sacred stories as powerful, truth-bearing stories, not historical reporting.*

With that in mind, let us take up Jesus' Apocalyptic Discourse in Matthew 24. It starts with "Jesus left the Temple." Though we tend to jump over that first verse to get to the center of the text, we need to stop there. The Temple, after all, represents the entire system, wrapped up in one great structure. Here's the entire first verse: "Jesus left the Temple, and as he was going away his disciples came up to draw his attention to the Temple buildings." The disciples are always doing things like that. It's the end of the Gospel, the twenty-fourth out of twenty-eight chapters, and they still haven't gotten the point! He's leaving the Temple and they're admiring its architecture.

The juxtaposition of phrases shouts at anyone who reads sacred literature well. The disciples are still rooted in the entire system the Temple represents. They're still marveling at the Temple structure, and Jesus' reply is, "You see all these stones? In truth I tell you, not a single stone here will be left on another" (Matthew 24:2b). "It's all going to fall apart. Will you stop putting your trust in it?"

The next verse gives us a hint: "And while he was sitting on the Mount of Olives, the disciples came and asked him when they were by themselves, 'Tell us, when is this going to happen, and what sign will there be of your coming and of the end of the world?'" (24:3). Again, there is a clever juxtaposition of phrases: When Christ's presence (*parousia*) is experienced, it *is* the end of the world as we have known it.

We normally read Matthew 24 over the last four Sundays of the church year to scare us and remind us that the world's going to end. But Matthew's message is communicated on both levels simultaneously: He's talking about the end of the world, but Matthew is also talking about the end of worlds. How appropriate that the last Sundays of the church year name the end of worlds before the new world comes in Advent and Christmas.

If you've ever gotten to a point in your life when you let go of a world, you understand this text. We cannot welcome the presence, the *parousia*, the full coming of Christ until we've let go of the old. We've lived under the illusion that we could have both: We could idolatrously worship this world order and, at the same time, say, "Thy Kingdom come." Yet we can't say, "Thy Kingdom come" unless we're willing to say, "My kingdom go." Remember this the next time you hear the apocalyptic readings in November. Don't be afraid to let the heavens be shaken (see Matthew 24:29) and to abandon the defense of your personal temple and cultural Jerusalem.

Shaking the Foundation: The Letting Go of Worlds

Unless we are willing to let go of our self-created ego worlds, we will not see the Reign of God in our midst. The ego, by nature, is conservative. It strives to conserve, to maintain itself. That translates into seeking to live within a comfort zone and staying there. Once we find that place where we feel secure, we may do anything to maintain it.

I remember an episode from the TV show *60 Minutes*. An investigative team was scrutinizing people in America who make bogus repairs. The investigators put secret markings inside of appliances, on parts that might be replaced during a repair. When they picked up the appliances from some repair shops, they could tell by taking off the appliance cover that the original parts were still in the appliance, even though the expensive repair bills listed replacement parts.

The investigators came back to the shops, cameras rolling, to present their evidence. "No, I didn't do that!" the repairmen claimed. "Here is proof!" the TV crew countered. "No, I didn't do that," the repairmen lied again. I sat there watching this in disbelief. Every single one of the repairmen denied the evidence before his eyes! It shows how capable we are of immense denial when the ego is involved.

Sadly, perhaps a more common example of this happens in homes where abuse is taking place. Often alcoholism is present too. Many women who finally come to crisis shelters, badly bruised, are in massive denial about their own abusers. They refuse to believe what is happening to them until they are so injured that they require medical help. Even then, many will continue to deny a pattern of abuse—"He just got carried away," they may say.

The Twelve Step programs have shown us how widespread this denial can be in our lives. We can become so self-protective we will lie through our teeth, as the saying goes. For the person—or the church or the society—caught in the trap of denial, security becomes an idol. We become incapable of loving and incapable of truth.

That world of denial and false security is the old world order Jesus is undercutting. Jesus talks about this undercutting in terms of salt and leaven. The Gospel is like a virus set loose in the world. There's no way to get the toothpaste back into the tube; there's no way to get the horse back in the barn; there's no way to undo Reign-of-God people. I see it wherever I go: people who know what's real, who have experienced the eternal and absolute. They know it's all relative and impermanent and refuse to worship any system. They are trapped—and it often feels like a trap!—in the truth.

In Matthew 24:4–8, Jesus says,

> Take care that no one deceives you, because many will come using my name and saying, "I am the Christ," and they will deceive many. You will hear of wars and rumors of wars; see that you are not alarmed, for this is something that must happen, but the end will not be yet. For nation will fight against nation, and kingdom against kingdom. There will be famines and earthquakes in various places. All this is only the beginning of the *birth pangs*. (emphasis added)

Jesus is presenting an image of something that is painful but is bringing about something better. The price of bringing something better is to go through the pain of birth. Do you think if we'd had a more feminine image of God that we would have understood creation as labor and giving birth? Much of patriarchal Christian interpretation has been trying to avoid pain, trying to avoid being poor, trying to avoid powerlessness. That's why we couldn't hear Jesus. If we had had an image of God as the great mother who is giving birth—as in Romans 8:22—I think history as process, pain, patience, and guided destiny would have come more naturally. As it is, we have seen history as a linear obstacle course, something to be conquered, exploited, and won.

A woman who has borne a child understands something I will never understand. I will never understand the innate connection between pain and life. When I give talks on male spirituality, I encourage men to consider this: Why were most tribal initiation rites for men? Why weren't they for women? Why did most peoples discover that men have to be *taught* about failure and suffering? Why did the vast majority of peoples create rites of passage, scarification, ordeals, vision quests, and circumcision for young men? It seems that men, in particular, must be taught that life is hard, that humans are not in control, that death is a reality.

Why not the women? Because a woman knows, in her body, that when bleeding happens there's something dying and yet something stirring. Some girls, surprised at the onset of menstruation, remember thinking they *were* dying. In her cycles and in childbirth, a woman can learn more about life than some men ever do. Women are able to make an early body connection that a man never makes. Along with their subservient position in most societies, women have a symbolic head start in understanding the Paschal Mystery of death and resurrection.

In the previous Apocalyptic Discourse quote, there was mention of famine and earthquakes. Of course, every time there is an earthquake, someone is trying to determine if this is the "biggie." We could regularly cook up evidence that now is the time for the apocalypse. We'll see, at the end of Matthew 24, that we shouldn't waste our time trying to figure that out: That isn't the point. The end is all the time. It's constant, and it never stops. This quaking of the earth is repeated by Matthew, both at the death of Jesus and the centurion's act of faith (27:51–54) and at the resurrection (28:2). In each case, it is now a new world and these acts are at the epicenter.

In the Discourse, a few verses further along, we read:

> Immediately after the distress of those days the sun will be darkened, the moon will not give its light, the stars will fall from the sky, and the powers of the heavens will be shaken. And then the sign of the Son of man will appear in heaven. Then, too, all the

peoples of the earth will beat their breasts, and they will see the Son of man coming on the clouds of heaven with power and great glory. (Matthew 24:29–30)

It's almost like a mythological description of depression. Have you ever had a day when it all doesn't make any sense? Emptiness has to precede fullness. Usually our old securities have to be wrested from us before we will move into the new. We seldom do it deliberately. Spirituality is always about letting go—not just in Christianity, but in Judaism, Islam, Hinduism, Buddhism, etc. All the great world religions, at their higher levels, teach the mystery and the art of letting go. We let go, and hopefully collapse back into our true self, into who we really are. The work of religion is to guide us on the path of the fall and onto the path of return. What Jesus is painting here with his words is a cosmic liturgy, a cosmic image of everything falling apart. Out of that emptiness comes the possibility of a new kind of fullness.

"Take the fig tree as a parable," he says. "As soon as its twigs grow supple and its leaves come out, you know that summer is near. So it is with you when you see all these things: know that the Son of Man is near, right at the gates. In truth I tell you, before this generation has passed away, all these things will have taken place" (Matthew 24:32–34).

It's interesting to note Jesus' style here. He doesn't quote Scripture; that's why his authority is not like the authority of the scribes and the Pharisees (see Matthew 7:29). He doesn't quote papal encyclicals. He most often uses *nature* as an authority. He points to clouds, sunsets, sparrows, lilies, corn in the field, leaves unfolding, several kinds of seeds, even oxen in a ditch!

Nature instructs us everywhere. Look and learn how to see. Look and see the rhythm, the seasons, the life and death of things. That's our teaching; that's creation's plan in front of us. The new world is constantly coming into being as the old world passes. *Nothing* lives in nature unless something else dies, and it often happens slowly and is unseen—unless we learn how to see.

Christians across the ages have tried to figure out why the world didn't end the way Jesus seemed to be saying it would. Remember, though, the Gospels were written after the Temple was already destroyed. Jesus uses Temple imagery, but the reason it's going to happen "before this generation passes away" is because it happens in every generation.

Jesus is incorrect chronologically or historically, but he is absolutely correct in terms of the soul. "Sky and earth will pass away, but my words will never pass away" (Matthew 24:35). "All you can do," Jesus goes on to say, "is *be ready!*" In fact, the next forty-four verses, leading up to the judgment scene, are all metaphors of readiness, awakening, vigilance, and cunning (Noah, peasants, property owners, stewards, bridesmaids, and entrepreneurs).

It is most unfortunate that, like naughty children, we have read these apocalyptic passages almost exclusively in terms of warning, threat, and dire prediction. That's a sad example of what happens when we read the sacred story mechanically instead of soulfully. Most of this chapter in Matthew is a call to be alert and awake, but we have heard it as Jesus telling us to be afraid—the exact thing against which he spoke.

Spirituality is about being ready. All the spiritual disciplines of our lives—prayer, study, meditation or ritual, religious vows—are there so we can break through to the eternal. Spirituality is about awakening the eyes, the ears, and the heart so we can see what's always been happening right in front of us.

One of the men's retreats I used to lead is on the hero's journey. I asked the men, "How do you prepare for being a hero? Do you go to hero school? Do you decide to do risky or dramatic things?" No, that will just get you into the ego. All you can do is be ready, and God will create your heroism—which won't even feel heroic to you.

I would tell people in discernment on retreats: Just ask the Lord to ready your heart. Don't try to build your own door or heroically create your own project. Don't even go search for the door through which you're supposed to enter. Just ask that when the door shows itself, you'll have the eyes to recognize it and the courage to walk through it. Other times, I would tell them, "Don't push the river. Just remain in the flow."

After reading this book and getting all fired up about Jesus' radical message, don't set out to open some big soup kitchen. (Unless you put down this book and the first thing someone tells you is, "We need a soup kitchen"—maybe *that* would be a beckoning!) Often, we do God's work for our own ego purposes. In reality, we probably all start there, and the wondrous truth is that God even uses such things to good purpose.

"So, stay awake," Jesus says, "because you do not know the day when your master is coming. You may be quite sure of this, that if the householder had known at what time of the night the burglar would come, he would have stayed awake and would not have allowed anyone to break through the wall of his house" (Matthew 24:42–43).

What a wonderful symbol of God as a burglar: the divine thief! Our patterns and character present a formidable armor against the Gospel. The only way the truth gets into any of our lives is by God's trickery, when our guard is down. (That's why we've got to listen to our dreams: because our character armor is down when we are sleeping.) Our operative God-image would probably be far more attractive and livelier if we had accepted such prankish or trickster relationships with God. The God of Jesus is clearly much more than a stern moralist or a divine police officer. Daringly, Jesus puts God "outside the law" as one who comes into our lives by stealth and cunning, the burglar who comes in the night and steals our soul in spite of ourselves!

God will always get at us when we're striving for a goal. The ego is moving straight ahead, into success and power, into good name, achievement, and all the other stupid things that we pursue. Then, once in a while, we glimpse out of the corner of our eye what really matters. Gotcha!

A Zen master frequently claps his hands to break the trance, the collective illusion of which we are all a part. Perhaps the bell we used to ring at the Consecration of the Mass was designed to do the same. We need to let go of the private dream for the dream of God.

Most of us live in the past, carrying our hurts, guilts, and fears. We have to face the pain we carry, lest we spend the rest of our lives running away from it or letting it run us. But the only place we will ever meet the real is *now, here*. It's the hardest place for us to live, the place where we're most afraid to live, because it feels so empty and boring. Now-here almost always feels like nowhere, and that's precisely where we must be.

Silence is what allows the old world order to become unnecessary, and we really don't know that until we are silent. I once had the luxury of a forty-seven-day contemplative retreat, where I escaped from this world order. I didn't need to depend upon it, believe it, or listen to it. I didn't play its games or carry out its roles. That is the historic meaning within so many mythologies of the hermit.

Jesus becomes a hermit when he goes off to the desert. John the Baptist lives in the desert. The desert is where we go to be apart from the world order as it is. It's where we simply stop being trapped in the world's addictive patterns. If we are addicted to the world's patterns or our own, we really need to go apart; otherwise, we will never stop sleepwalking.

It makes me wonder how many people today are going to get out of the trap. With earphones playing music all day and social media in front of us all the time, will we ever know what the real is? I'm not talking here about who's going to heaven and who's not going to heaven. That language seems to cause more harm than good. In fact, it would be better to get rid of that language completely. It really doesn't help us understand what Jesus was up to. We've got to know that what Jesus is talking about, first and foremost, is how we enter into the real *now*. Jesus gives us real eyes to realize where the Real lies. (Say that last sentence aloud—that might help you remember!)

The Mustard Seed/Weed Parable of the Reign of God

It's very hard for us to understand our world without a philosophy of progress. Yet I think Jesus lived in such a world. Jesus realizes that what he's talking about is going to come about rather modestly. That's hard for us to hear, because we've been raised in a world of progress and goals. We all have been loaded with expectations about how we will grow up and become certain things, whether domestic or professional. We think we are what we do. Fortunately, our inherent Christ nature is not a goal to be achieved, but an inheritance to be recognized.

Jesus doesn't think in modern Western terms. His parables, particularly from Matthew 13, make this very clear. This section of Matthew is called the Parabolic Discourse. The Reign of God is Jesus' message. He never describes it conceptually. He walks around it and keeps giving images of the Real. This is the classic pattern of the spiritual teacher. Only those who are ready and seeking will normally understand. Others will read those images as innocuous aphorisms. Scripture scholars in recent decades have broadened our understanding of these parables through their research into Jesus' times.

For example, "The Reign of Heaven is like a mustard seed which a man took and sowed in his field. It is the smallest of all the seeds, but when it has grown it is the biggest of shrubs [which isn't really true] and becomes a tree, so that the birds of the air can come and shelter in its branches" (Matthew 13:31–32).

The mustard seed is very small and insignificant. Pliny the Elder (23/24–79 CE), a contemporary of Jesus, wrote a big book called *Natural History*, in which he described all the plants that were known in the Mediterranean world. He wrote only two things about the mustard plant.

It's medicinal, so it did have some value. But he advised not to plant it because it tends to take over the entire garden. It is a weed that cannot be stopped.

Those would have been the two images upon which Jesus was clearly building: "What I'm describing for you is therapeutic—it's life, it's healing, it's medicinal—but it's like a weed." What a shocking image! It's like a virus: "I'm planting a weed in the world. I'm going to talk about unexpected things like nonviolence and the simple life, but I've planted them and they're going to take over. The old world is over. I don't know if it's going to take two thousand years or four thousand years before you get the point, but I've planted what I know is eternal truth in the world and it's going to take over."

But there's opposition: the birds. We city folks picture the birds coming down into the branches: "Cute little bluebirds. Won't that be nice!" But to any farmer, birds are a negative image, because they eat up all the seeds. Birds are the enemy! Farmers don't want birds in their fields. So, Jesus is saying, "I'm planting something that's like a weed—a therapeutic one, but a weed nonetheless. It's going to grow with great difficulty because there will be all kinds of opposition. But it will prevail. It will eventually take over the whole garden."

That's Jesus' hope, but do you see what patient hope that is? He didn't see it happen in his lifetime. Remember, from the beginning, Jesus proclaimed this Reign of God—the Real—in a world where 98 percent of people were poor. They were all, except for the Romans, an occupied people. The vast majority of them were enslaved. Religion was highly corrupt. And still, in the midst of that, he dared to announce the present Reign of God! He dared to say, "You can live the new reality right now." That's most extraordinary.

The word for living that way, living in the in-between times, is *faith*. Get rid of every thought you've had about faith, if that's possible. Forget, for the moment, about believing in the Immaculate Conception or the pope.

They're not what Jesus is talking about. He's talking about the grace and the freedom to live God's dream for the world *now*—while not rejecting the world as it is. That's a mighty tension that is not easily resolved.

Remember this: There are always two worlds. The world as it operates is power; the world as it should be is love. The secret of Reign-of-God life is how we can live in both—simultaneously. The world as it is will always be built on power, ego, and success. Yet, we also must keep our eyes intently on the world as it should be—what Jesus calls the Reign of God. Power apart from love leads to brutality, but love that does not engage with power is mere sentimentality. A lot of Christians today are still trapped in one or the other.

Images of Hiddenness and Timing

Jesus told another parable right after the Mustard Seed: "The Reign of Heaven is like the yeast a woman took and mixed in with three measures [about fifty pounds!] of flour till it was leavened all through" (Matthew 13:33b). If any of you have been to San Francisco and tasted sourdough bread, you might have the correct image here. Leaven is not the nice little package of yeast we buy at the grocery store. That's our modern, sanitized version of what people have known for centuries as leaven.

Leaven actually evokes an image of corruption. (Thus the bread of the Passover had to be new and *un*leavened.) Sourdough is set in the corner until it gets bubbly and smelly. Then Jesus says a woman took and hid this seemingly corrupt thing inside the flour and it was enough to leaven, eventually, the entire fifty pounds! Clearly, the three measures of flour is a deliberately large amount—to give us hope.

Jesus is content, it seems, not to be the whole loaf, but instead the smelly leaven that we put inside. That's who we are, and that's what we can feel like when we start living the Gospel—too full of leaven for anything else. "Why don't I believe in all these other things? Why am I not excited about the elections? Every time we change presidents, people think it's going to make a big difference: Why can't I get excited about it?" We have been salted, leavened, and enlightened by a much bigger truth; that's why.

The point in the next two parables about the treasure and the pearl is the same:

> The Reign of Heaven is like treasure hidden in a field which someone has found; he hides it again, goes off in his joy, sells everything he owns, and buys the field. Again, the Reign of Heaven is like a merchant looking for fine pearls; when he finds one of great value, he goes and sells everything he owns and buys it. (Matthew 13:44–45)

The Reign of God is hidden and yet available. God is perfectly hidden and perfectly revealed in every moment. The Reign of God is an open secret. Can we hold both of those ideas together? "These are just flesh-and-blood people in my life, aren't they? These are just flowers. This is just a table, isn't it?" God is perfectly hidden here; there is no way we see God. But God is also perfectly revealed in every moment. Clearly, this is an invitation to take this material world seriously. Physical creation is both the hiding place and the revealing place of God!

Matthew ends the Parabolic Discourse with Jesus asking, "'Have you understood all these?' They say, 'Yes'" (13:51)—but it's so obvious they haven't because we still haven't gotten the message two thousand years later! It's still hidden, subversive, and not the way we want to see things.

The final verses of chapter 13 are Matthew's signature: "Well then, every scribe who becomes a disciple of the Reign of Heaven is like a householder who brings out from his storeroom new things as well as old" (13:52). We're not sure who really wrote this Gospel, but it probably was a converted scribe. Some scholars think this was his way of getting himself in there and describing his task.

This scribe we call Matthew tried to bring out of the same storehouse things both new and old and put them together. That, I believe, is the work of the "magician," the work of spirituality, the work of Jesus. It creates a new, symbolic universe at the dangerous level of imagination. Jesus is involved in a war of myths. The ultimate battle for the soul is to change the way we imagine our reality.

In the Parabolic Discourse, Jesus tells us to withdraw our allegiance from a world of bigness, clarity, immediacy, looking good, and security (the old order) and to see life instead as smallness, patience, humility, inner wisdom, and risk-taking (always new and rare).

Once our symbolic world changes, once we're converted in the gut, we are trapped in the truth and can never forget it.

We can no longer take some things seriously. The Sermon on the Mount—indeed, all the Gospel—creates for us that new, symbolic universe.

chapter three

Finding the Jesus Who Preached the Sermon

We say "Jesus Christ" as if Christ is Jesus' last name. That's because we're so comfortable with putting the two identities together. We could say that Jesus is the historical man of Nazareth who walked this earth, and the Christ is the great archetypal identity that is put on Jesus, the one who leads us to the Father. Both identities are true: Our faith as Christians is in Jesus Christ, the historical man Jesus *and* the cosmic Christ.

In this book, I'm largely emphasizing Jesus, because until we get back to "Jesus before Christianity," in the words of Dominican Albert Nolan,[8] we don't have anything solid upon which to build. We keep creating fantasy Jesuses—who can be molded into whomever we want Jesus to be. We've got to go back to the historical Jesus to rebuild our foundations. What did Jesus really teach and what are the later developments from the tradition and from the church?

As we name how history and culture have shaped our understanding of Jesus, we've got to admit the biases of each century. What problems of the first century was Jesus addressing? Why did his contemporaries see Jesus in a certain way? Are the questions of Jesus the perennial human questions?

We moderns are coming along after two thousand years with accretion upon accretion—they can feel like barnacles on a ship. Will the true Jesus please stand up? Fortunately, there's been much exciting scholarship in recent decades. We are learning to be honest about the historical Jesus, to let him speak for himself through the Scriptures.

Inspired Biases

Two Different Pictures of Jesus

Synoptic Gospels (Matthew, Mark, and Luke)	The Gospel of John
Start with John the Baptist, infancy stories, perhaps birth.	Starts with cosmic creation, no birth or infancy narrative.
Jesus speaks like a Semitic sage, in parables and aphorisms.	Jesus speaks in long, dense, theological narratives.
Jesus is a lay teacher and holy man.	Jesus is a mystic philosopher.
Jesus is an exorcist.	Jesus performs no exorcisms.
The "Kingdom" or "Reign of God" is Jesus' constant theme.	Jesus is announcing himself in his major proclamations.
Mostly action and explanation of action; little self-analysis by Jesus.	Jesus has created an entire theology and justification for everything he is and does.
Jesus is unfailingly on the side of the poor, the oppressed, and the outsider. They are often praised above the believers and establishment leaders.	The poor and oppressed are hardly mentioned. In fact, "we" are good while "Jews" and unbelievers are bad.
Whole story is about one year of adult ministry.	Public ministry lasts three years.
Extended last supper, passion, death, and resurrection accounts.	Foot-washing replaces story of bread and wine. Highly stylized theology of passion, death, and resurrection.

I hope that this quick overview of the obvious helps us to see that we have had varied theologies about Jesus from the beginning. Both pictures presented here are accepted as "orthodox" and true presentations of the only Jesus we know: the historical and transcendent figure who formed the faith of these writers and these communities. This is the Living Jesus who inspired a living Bible.

There is no such thing as an *entirely objective* viewpoint on anything. Every viewpoint is a view from a point. Intelligent and faith-filled reading of inspired texts merely takes that point seriously so it can better understand what Jesus was trying to say *in that original context*. His story is also our story.[9]

Modern Jesus Scholarship

Modern scholars are looking at the Gospels with new eyes, trying to piece together how much actually comes from the life of Jesus and how much is the interpretation of the early church.

Almost none of John's Gospel is considered by mainstream scholars today to be directly from Jesus. Most of what Jesus says in John's Gospel are words put in Jesus' mouth by this community around the year 100 or 110 CE. It is not corroborated by other Gospels or writings, to our knowledge. That doesn't make it wrong. The point in studying the Christian Scriptures is this: The story is *always true*—and sometimes it really happened! That is the nature of all sacred scriptures.

The written Gospels are the unfolding of the story as those who loved and followed Jesus understood his words seventy or eighty years later. Those stories are presented by the faith communities—in their context, given their biases, given their problems and their needs. We can clearly see that's true by noting how the Gospels contradict one another. The Gospels are not presenting the historical Jesus, for the most part. Then again, they are not entirely ahistorical either. Jesus was certainly real and historical, but as his story was told many decades after his death, it was filled with variety and interpretation.

If we are not willing to live with that, we've got nothing else upon which to build, because that's all we have: early followers' reconstructions of narrative, once or twice removed from the historical Jesus but grounded in the early Christian community. That demands of Christians a great act of faith in what we call inspiration or the guidance of the Holy Spirit. We believe that the Spirit was guiding this community as it developed its belief in the historical Jesus. That's how we get from a peasant proclaiming the Reign of God in Galilee through mythic imagery to the year 100, where we have the divine Son of God walking around, calling himself by God's name, "I-AM-WHO-I-AM."

Only in John's Gospel does Jesus say "I AM." Jesus doesn't say it in Mark, Matthew, or Luke. The faith there is still unfolding and finding appropriate words—as, indeed, it still is today.

Yet, that doesn't mean John's Gospel isn't true. It means John's Gospel tells us what the Spirit in the Johannine community had come to recognize by the year 100. They have what we call a "high" or developed Christology. They have come to understand Jesus as the Christ (the Anointed One), as the Son of the Father, and as the Divine Logos (Word of God).

Much of what is in the Gospels results from new situations and new problems being encountered by the early Christian communities. The Jesus story was remembered and passed on verbally over a period of thirty to seventy years before the Gospels were written. This early preaching is called the *kerygma*. It was the first language used by believers to describe their faith experience of Jesus. For almost thirty years, it was largely oral.

Put yourself in the sandals of an apostle. You're standing in front of a group of people, you're presenting Jesus, and you've got to make this Jesus fit this crowd, so you sort of embroider the words a little. That's certainly been the way of preachers throughout history, including this one! When I preach, I've got to make it so twenty-first-century Americans can understand Jesus. I put another level onto it. A preacher cannot *not* do that. *There is no such thing as uninterpreted fact in the human world.*

This adaptation of the Jesus story to address new situations comes from the pre-biblical church. It may be unsettling to some, but the church *did* exist before the Bible. The church had a source of authority before it had the Bible: the Christian community itself, its belief, its oral tradition. That's what Roman Catholics have held onto, for good and for ill. We believe there are, in fact, three sources of revelation: Experience, Scripture, *and* Tradition.

Now, when Martin Luther (1483–1546) comes along, he says *sola scriptura*, "Scripture alone." Of course, Luther didn't admit his own biases. Luther had a lot of tradition that he didn't realize he was carrying. Since there is no such thing as a bias-free or value-free position, we need to be aware of that bias, in ourselves and others. Again, every viewpoint is a view from a point.

That's not to denigrate Luther; that's just to recognize we can't be *sola scriptura*. It's impossible. We necessarily come from a culture, from a temperament, from an economic worldview, a social worldview. Luther did too. As much as he declared he was only appealing to the authority of Scripture, it's obvious in hindsight that many of the things he chose to notice in Scripture were in response to his own issues.

Please don't underestimate Luther's contribution, though. Many of the practices of the Roman Catholic Church were misguided, and Luther, priest and Bible scholar, correctly recognized that. Catholicism eventually dealt with them, although sometimes in a reactionary way, during the Counter-Reformation.

What Luther did with Scripture is what the Roman Catholic hierarchy does, and what you and I do too, and that's OK. Anyone who is serious about understanding the Christian Scriptures has to move beyond the way most of us were taught to read the Bible. We have to become more historically aware and self-critical, admitting that human beings wrote the Bible and human beings have been interpreting it for centuries. Isn't it even more wondrous to believe that inspiration is in *us* too? The Spirit is guiding human history, not just the written words.

Paul and Luther likely had similar personalities. So, Luther went to Paul to find what he needed, because both of them were struggling with the same issue: "I want to be a good boy and I can't. I want to be perfect and I can't. Ah, God loves me unconditionally—hallelujah!" Luther jumped up and Paul jumped up: "God loves me unconditionally!" But then, they made that point the whole Gospel, and every emphasis of one point is necessarily a deemphasis of another.

Therefore, they both miss almost everything Jesus says about social justice and about so many other issues that most concerned Jesus himself. I don't mean to belittle the experience of unconditional love. We need to have it too, for all of this to make sense. But we can't just fill people with enthusiasm every Friday night by reconvincing them of God's unconditional love. Finally, we have to go out into the vineyards and marketplaces of the world and preach "good news to the nations" (see Matthew 28:19) and not just to individuals. Paul was, of course, doing this with his emphasis on community and church order.

Beyond repeating actual sayings of Jesus and adapting these for early pastoral situations, the Gospels include much that seems to be the outright creation of new sayings and stories by the earliest Christian communities. In these new sayings and stories, the communities document their understanding of Jesus—and, in some cases, we must admit, the new context changes the content of Jesus' original message. The Gospel writers are clearly making a new point. Thus, the same healing story will be remembered in three or four different ways.

We try to trust that even those new points are good points for us because they were good points for Matthew's community, for example, in the year 90. That is when Matthew's Gospel was put to papyrus: about sixty years after Jesus' death and resurrection. The self-criticism and self-congratulation that we find *in the final text* is, in fact, the exact kind of narrative that we need—to encourage us to go and do likewise! That is also probably the most helpful form of inspiration. It profits no one to say that only the historical event, exactly as it happened, is the source of divine guidance.

Three Sources for Matthew

Matthew's Gospel, as we have it today, was compiled in the early years of the church from three sources. The first of the sources is what we think of as Mark's Gospel. That Gospel could have been written as early as 60 CE, but perhaps as late as 70 CE.

Imagine the difference between 1980 and 2020. That forty-year span means a generation or longer after Jesus' death and resurrection before we get the first written Gospel. That's why it's foolish ever to look upon the Gospels as biographies of Jesus. They're masterpieces of theology, of mythology (in the best sense of that term), of history (in the best sense of that term)—but not our twenty-first-century rational, scientific understanding of history.

The second source is often called the Q document—Q for the German word *quelle*, meaning "source." We don't have an "original" of this anymore, but we surmise that it must have existed. From careful study and comparison, we see that Matthew and Luke must draw upon some common source outside of themselves that we no longer have. That's the Q document.

The third source is tradition and the perceptions of Matthew's communities—the problem he is trying to solve—and the oral fragments that have come down to them. This is sometimes called the M source.

With all that background, we can look at how the Gospels were written. Stage one is the historical event itself, to which there are very few, if any, eyewitnesses (for example, Jesus and Satan in the desert; Matthew 4:1–11). Yet the Gospels are not concerned with conveying an accurate biography of Jesus. That's our hang-up. The Gospels are about telling the *meaning* of Jesus, and his effect on their lives. This is personal testimony, "good news" more than empirical facts.

Then we have stage two: very specific situations in each of the communities. The Synoptic Gospels (Matthew, Mark, and Luke) look at things in somewhat the same way, with variations for these situations. (*Syn op* means "to see the same.") Scholars compare similar passages and identify how each passage was slightly changed. They look for what was included and what was left out. That reveals the biases. That's how we can assume, for example, that Matthew was writing to a middle-class community and Luke was writing to a poor community: because we see the kinds of stories they skipped, the kinds of phrases they added, the kinds of words they included or excluded. All that reveals the bias or pastoral concern of each author.

The written Gospels as we have them come from a third stage, built upon the first and the second. They were composed by evangelists and their disciples according to the needs and understandings of their time and place, decades after the historical life of Jesus.

Yet, the four Gospels can only be understood in relation to all three stages: the historical event, the way each of the early Christian communities interpreted it, and how the final author wrote it down. Our act of faith—and it *is* an act of faith—is that all three stages are, in fact, divine revelation: God acting in history to reveal *who God is* and what happens when God encounters humanity. The text is a "text in travail,"[10] revealing the patterns and processes, not just the conclusions. This is why Scripture is such a fruitful source of transformation for every age, but also very open to misuse by those who don't enter into the travail themselves.

For a believing Christian, both the life of the Word of God and the text of the word of God are illuminated by the process of historical reconstruction. Again, I want to state that I consider such a style of revelation a plus and not a deficiency. Now we can expect God's revelation in our history too—not just back in the "good old days."

Though it came from three sources, the Gospel of Matthew was not haphazardly written. The author clearly had a sense of outline, as do most good writers today. Matthew's Gospel is too well-ordered not to have an underlying plan and intended audience. Our job is to accept his agenda, not to force Matthew into ours. Then we will have *teaching*.

First of all, we have the two bookends: the Prologue and the Epilogue. The Prologue is what we call chapter 1. (Chapter and verse numbers were not added until the Middle Ages.) When Matthew wrote, he didn't know that he was writing a book of the Bible. He was just writing the Good News for the Christian community.

Matthew's Gospel differs from Mark's. Mark's Gospel is basically an account of the passion, death, and resurrection of Jesus. One gets the sense that all Mark's authors really cared about was revealing the great mystery of death and resurrection. They added some simple stories of healings and teachings up front, but the passion, death, and resurrection narrative is central. Jesus stops talking. He knows we're going to miss the point in words. We won't believe it unless he walks through it himself and says, "This is the way through: crucifixion and resurrection."

Rather than focus so much on the passion, death, and resurrection of Jesus, Matthew composes a Gospel of five books. Each book combines a series of narratives and sermons. The narrative, in most cases, prepares us for the sermon that follows.

Jesus' Worldview

The sermon on which we're going to spend the most time is the inaugural sermon, the Sermon on the Mount (Matthew 5–7). Recent scholarship reaffirms that this is as close as we can get to Jesus' original message; it seems to be the heart of the teaching of the historical Jesus. It surely represents the style of a Jewish peasant layman: aphorisms, stories, and parables that are provocative, quotable, often short, and memorable. Very frequently, they cut against the grain of conventional wisdom, while focusing on a God who is good and can be trusted.

Matthew's narratives are usually collections of healing stories, exorcisms, and confrontations of growing hostility between Jesus and the establishment. All this finally builds to a kind of climax with the scene in the Temple that leads to Jesus' passion, death, and raising up.

We've tended to soften Jesus' conflict with the system ever since the church became an establishment. The year that we choose for that transition is the year 313. That is the year of the Edict of Milan, or the Constantinian Revolution. It was then that the church changed dramatically—and changed sides dramatically. Up until that time, the church was, by and large, of the underclass. It identified with the oppressed and the poor. The church itself was still being oppressed and Christians were being thrown to the lions. It reads history from the catacombs—literally from underground, which always gives us a different perspective than "those found in palaces," which is exactly how Jesus distinguishes between religious leaders and his cousin John (see Matthew 11:8).

Emperor Constantine thought he was doing Christians a favor in 313 when he made Christianity the established religion. Yet it might be the single most unfortunate thing that happened to Christianity. Once we moved from the bottom of society to the top, we developed a new film over our eyes, and we couldn't see anything that showed Jesus in confrontation with the establishment. We *became* the establishment. Clear teaching on issues of greed, control, powerlessness, nonviolence, and simplicity were moved to the sidelines, if not actually countermanded.

We'll see, as we get into the Sermon on the Mount, that Jesus intended for us to take the low road. He intended us to operate from the minority position, from the position of an "immoral" minority much more than the "moral majority." When we are protecting our self-image as moral, superior, or "saved" persons, we always lose the truth. The daring search for God—the common character of all religion—is replaced with the search for personal certitude and control.

As long as the church was underground in some sense, as long as we operated from a minority position, we had greater access to the truth, to the Gospel, and to Jesus. In our time, we have to find a way to disestablish ourselves, to identify with our powerlessness instead of our power, our dependence instead of our independence, and our communion instead of our individualism. Unless we understand that, the Sermon on the Mount isn't going to make any sense.

As soon as people are comfortable, they don't want any truth outside their comfort zone. People who are at the top of the system normally will vote "conservative" because once you're at the top of a system, you want to conserve the system as it is. You're enjoying its fruits; why would you want to change it? Yet those who are not enjoying the fruits of the system are always longing and thirsting for the coming of the Reign of God, for something more. They are not as likely to vote for the status quo, which is invariably built on those bottom lines of money, power, and God-talk. For the millennial vision, the Messianic promise, life has to be more than this. The Gospel always keeps us on that side of the question, in a state of longing and thirsting for God. Grace seems to create a void inside of us that only grace can fill.

I believe that Jesus is the great reconciler. Picture two lines, one going vertically, the other going horizontally: That's the cross. Pioneer psychologist Carl Jung stated that Jesus was killed in an "agonizing suspension between irreconcilable opposites."[11] Whenever we try to hold opposite energies together—liberal/conservative, masculine/feminine, right/wrong, black/white, anything that's conflictive—we are going to get crucified. When viewing the cross, picture a collision of opposites, the coming together of opposing energies, both of which invariably think they're the whole truth.

Paul saw this clearly, thirty years after Jesus died: "God wanted all fullness to be found in him and through him to reconcile all things to him, everything in heaven and everything on earth, by making peace through his death on the cross" (Colossians 1:19–20).

Bridge builders, including Jesus, usually start building a bridge from one side. A bridge can't be built from the middle, as any engineer will tell you. We must choose a starting point. What the Gospel is saying, pure and simple, is that wherever we're going to start building our bridge, we had better start from the side of powerlessness, not power. Because if we start on the side of power, we will stay there forever. We really won't build any bridges.

Yet we can't stay on the side of powerlessness. We discover the true meaning of power as we build the bridge to it, and Jesus will redefine the nature of power for us. So, we must be bridge builders. We must pay the price in our body for building those bridges (see Colossians 1:24) and know we'll be abused and misquoted from both sides. But the necessary starting point for building the bridge of the Gospel is from the side of powerlessness, either political powerlessness or our personal powerlessness—and preferably both. If we start there, we have a good chance of coming to the truth. It will always be a conversion, a turning around, to get back to what some call "beginner's mind."

Let's put that in the back of our hearts and minds. Maybe it will set the stage for getting into the text. Let that context prepare us to understand why Jesus is going to say such nonsensical, ridiculous things. Because powerlessness, as best as I can read the Gospels, is the worldview of Jesus. Without emptiness, there can be no fullness. Without a beginner's curiosity, there can be no learning. Only those who possess nothing can be entrusted with everything. In the first two chapters of this book, we saw that Jesus of Nazareth challenged his disciples to accept an entirely new system of values, a new world order. In this chapter, I hope, I have explained what some of those values are. In the remainder of this book, we will be reading the Bible in perhaps a new way. Now we will turn to a detailed look at the society Jesus was challenging, and an explanation of why Matthew tells the story the way he does.

chapter four
·····················

Understanding the Social Order

Most societies create social classes, consciously or unconsciously. Like it or not, it gives great comfort to the psyche to at least know where we stand. Societies with obvious social classes tend to create less widespread discontent than societies like America's, which falsely claims not to have such classes.

People tend to compare themselves with other people within their class. Construction workers tend to compare themselves to other construction workers, intellectuals to other intellectuals, and so on. *Our* worldview, however, tends toward across-the-board envy, competition, and comparison. Many of us go through life preoccupied with the hope of moving into a higher class. We have the illusion we could make tons of money if only we were smart or lucky enough.

No wonder so many people in American society are anxious! The ego only knows itself by comparisons, and comparing is a losing game because our reference points are always changing. We are building on sand (see Matthew 7:24–27).

To understand the social order Jesus was challenging, we must understand the class system of agrarian society. At the outset, I would like to express my indebtedness to John Dominic Crossan and his book *The Historical Jesus: The Life of a Mediterranean Jewish Peasant* for his rendition of much of the scholarship that follows.[12] Please do not construe my use of Crossan's valuable scholarship on the life and times of Jesus as any kind of endorsement of his ultimate conclusions, which have drawn fire from many critics. I am not relying on his conclusions in this book, only his accurate picture of Jesus' culture.

During Jesus' time, most of the world lived in agrarian societies. Gerhard E. Lenski (1924–2015), in his book *Power and Privilege: A Theory of Social Stratification,* identified nine classes of agrarian society.[13] At the top of society was the ruler. The ruler was one person, in a class by themselves, usually the king or queen. In most agrarian societies, the ruler controlled or had complete access to at least 25—and often 50—percent of the gross national product. Everything went to aggrandizing that person.

From our perspective, we might ask, "Wasn't that evil?" But, underneath the enormous inequity, there were actually some positive aspects. Without condoning it too much, we can note that having a ruling class gave people much more social security—in the real meaning of that term—than people have now. People knew where they stood and what their role was.

In a more rigid class society, no one would compare themselves to the ruler. He (or she) is the ruler, and is *supposed* to have the lion's share of the gross national product. People outside the ruling class accept what they have.

The second class in agrarian society—about 1 percent—was the governing class: the bureaucrats, nobles, and officials who surrounded the ruler. They received, as a group, at least an additional 25 percent of the gross national product. This 1 percent and the ruler, then, owned at least half, and often 75 percent, of all the goods and services in the society.

Then there was the retainer class, those who maintained the system. These were lower-class bureaucrats: the military, scribes, and teachers in Jesus' society. They comprised about 5 percent of the population. Retainers serve the political elite. They are the secretaries and soldiers. They want to keep their jobs, so they fight for the ruler and the 1 percent who have the money. Retainers have some degree of education and know-how.

The retainer class in Jesus' society merits a closer look, before we examine the other classes. The scribes were in that class. You may have noticed that in so many of the miracle stories and the exorcisms, the scribes are upset with Jesus. Why? Because he is taking away their job security.

If we want to understand the import of any of Jesus' miracles, we read who he's talking to at the beginning and who is upset at the end. Normally, the people who are upset at the end have just seen their job made unnecessary. Scribes, the equivalent of lawyers today, were those who, since the days of Leviticus and Numbers, had manufactured very complex systems of laws that created a demand for their expertise. Scribes helped people to wade through the system—and, of course, to wade through with them you had to pay them something.

In Israel at the time of Jesus, church and state were one. The laws were largely tied up with religion. For example, there were very clear rules on how a person with leprosy is to be made clean and what the person must do. There were clear rules about how a woman must be treated. So, when Jesus goes walking around the countryside, touching people and saying, "Be made clean!" that's a subversive action. "You can't do this!" a scribe might have said. "You've just ignored the whole legal system." (Read: "You've just taken away our benefits!")

With that understanding, it becomes more obvious why most of the Jewish leadership cooperated in having Jesus killed. Jesus was making God too accessible. He ignored the debt codes, the purity codes, and the honor-and-shame system that held the whole thing together. We'll take a closer look at that toward the end of this chapter.

The governing class, retainers, and rulers were, of course, almost entirely against Jesus—with some precious and beautiful exceptions. Matthew, for example, describes himself as a former scribe who is converted, which is why he understands the message so well. He was a man of the system.

The merchant class comes next. That class was very small in agrarian society. In Jesus' lifetime, it was certainly less than 5 percent. It wasn't until the time of Saint Francis (the thirteenth century) that the merchant class began to take over. Today, merchants control the world, but a dominant merchant class is a new phenomenon, as is an industrial society based on consuming and producing. Since the beginning, most people on this earth have been farmers.

The last of the five classes who comprise the establishment was the priestly class. They were landowners then, just as they have been, in one way or another, throughout history. We'll zoom up fifteen centuries for a quick look at the situation during the Reformation to illustrate the point. At the time of the Reformation, religious orders owned more than half of Europe. The serfs worked for the monks. (I can understand why my spiritual father Francis forbade Franciscans to own land. For some reason, the religious establishment always gets into real estate.) The Reformation was more about politics than theology. It happened because of the moral and economic corruption of so much of the church and because the church owned so much land. The priestly class was tied up with land and buildings in Jesus' time too.

Besides the five ruling classes in agrarian society, there were lower classes. They comprised at least 80 percent of the society. Those who farmed the land were the peasant class. Very often, they were tenant farmers—someone else owned the land. That's why so many of the parables of Jesus are about landlords and tenants. The folks he taught could lose their livelihood in a moment. They were at the whim of the ruling class and the landlords. *Two-thirds* of what they produced was spent on rent, taxes, and tolls.

Imagine surviving as a peasant in a year of drought. After you've given two-thirds away to the ruling class and to those to whom you're subservient, you still have to save enough of your grain for seed for next year so you can plant again. And, of course, you have to save enough to feed your cattle or other livestock. Whatever tiny bit is left is all you and your children have to live on for a year. That's how most poor people have lived since the beginning of time. In two-thirds of the world it is still much that way today.

Jesus came from this lower group. He was a Galilean peasant. Some new studies even question whether Jesus was literate. Jesus was a poor, simple man who knew how peasants struggled. We must understand that to understand his message more fully. Most of the people he taught were in the same situation. Jesus and his audience understood each other.

Within the peasant class there were subclasses. Our seventh class was the artisans. Comprising about 5 percent, they were skilled workers, such as carpenters, who were recruited from the ranks of dispossessed peasants. They always had to depend upon a patron. The artisans were gifted, yet they remained poor.

The eighth class was comprised of the people deemed unclean by reason of origin or of occupation. For example, in Jewish society, people who took care of pigs were considered unclean. The "unclean" still exist in all societies today, although the label is more subtle and often unadmitted. (Poor people, people of color, LGBTQIA+, old people, people with disabilities, non-Christians, foreigners—all these are the modern version of unclean groups in Western society.) Jesus has a great deal of contact with this group.

But the unclean were not so low as the totally expendable class. This ninth class might have been as much as 5 to 10 percent of all peasants. These expendable ones had to live by their wits. Call them criminals, or, if they lived on the charity of others, call them beggars. They were the unemployed or the unemployable. Lepers were often in this class, although sometimes they'd be a notch higher, in the unclean class.

The word Matthew uses for the poor in spirit, for example, at the beginning of the Sermon on the Mount, is *ptochoi*. It refers not just to peasants, but to these very bottom classes: the destitute. Jesus is saying, "You're at the very bottom of the heap, but I want you to know you've got freedom there and I'm going to help you find it." He's talking to the least of the brothers and sisters, as we will see in Matthew 25—the lowest of the peasant class. Many of Jesus' comments about the poor are about these last two classes, the unclean and the expendable people. The farmer still had his land. He was dirt poor, but he at least had something to fall back on.

Before moving on, we should note a sad connection to our own society. Today, it's this final class that is growing so quickly: the expendable people who are unemployed and unemployable. "There's no way we need you," we say, in effect. "We will undereducate you, undertrain you, and undervalue you. We throw you in prisons. We even hope you kill one another. We hope the drugs and guns will allow you to kill one another because we can't fit you into our definition of success, our definition of reality." Yet it was the people at the bottom of society for whom Jesus most consistently showed concern. They seem to be the measure of how well we understand the new world order.

Who Is Your Patron?

The society of Jesus' day was also a society of patronage. This kind of society has lasted in Mexico, for example, to a high degree, even to our day. It's one of the reasons behind conflict between Mexico and the United States. In a society of patronage, you are not defined by what you have or what you know, but *who* you know. Everything depends on your connections. If you don't have connections, you just don't get anywhere.

That's why many of us will feel so lost, for example, if we go to Mexico: We have no connections there. We are powerless without connections. Most of the Mediterranean world was that way, and the cultures founded by the Mediterranean world still are. Italian and Spanish societies retain patronage to some degree, although northern European society has lost it.

Older Roman Catholics may understand this idea easily. The idea of the patron saint came out of the Mediterranean world. In a patronage society, someone has to stand between the individual and the overlord. The patron saint is the same idea.

My community, the Franciscans, has been working with the Native Americans in the pueblos of New Mexico for centuries. Yet one of the things we haven't been able to change is the position of Jesus in the grand scheme of things. In the hierarchy, Jesus is third, at best. First is the Great Spirit: God. Then comes the patron saint! That's why pueblos have the big dances on the feast days of the patron saints. It's the pueblo's individual connection with the Big One. Santa Clara, San Ildefonso, or Santo Domingo (to name a few examples) is on your side. We older Catholics all had a patron saint who was up there batting for us, who was our connection.

When you've grown up as a peasant in a society of patronage, you're nothing. You're insignificant, and you've got to use your connections, your patron. The loyalty in both directions is often admirable, and need not be judged merely by our supposed democratic standards.

That relationship of little person to patron—wherever it shows up in history—grows inevitably into a system of honor and shame. The little person must show honor and respect to the patron, and the patron has a moral obligation to take care of the little one who pays honor. There are obligations on both sides. In the West, this became the feudal system that lasted for centuries.

We don't really understand that system anymore. We have immediate access; we don't need patrons. Protestantism embraces patronless theology because, in many ways, it was a reaction against corrupt feudal institutions. Protestants as a whole don't understand Mary or the saints; Protestantism doesn't want any go-betweens.

Jesus himself is the go-between, though, for all who call themselves Christian. That's the Christ image, who stands as the mediating symbol between us and God. Jesus says, "No one can come to the Father except through me" (John 14:6b). "Look at me and you'll know what God is like." Jesus is, in effect, our Great Patron, who stands between us and God. He tells us we can trust God because God is like him. "Anyone who has seen me has seen the Father" (John 14:9b). Daringly, he says, "I am the gate" (John 10:7b).

All this is background for understanding the Sermon on the Mount. Until we understand patronage society, we won't understand a lot of the Sermon on the Mount, or much of the rest of Jesus' teaching. In many ways, Jesus is taking away the broker that society established. He's telling the people that God is totally accessible, that God is available in reality itself, in experience itself, in the world of graced relationships. The Reign of God is in our midst (see Luke 17:21). We don't need to go through the brokerage system in Jerusalem or worship the emperor in Rome. What a threat to the system!

The system responded by killing him.

We've grown up with the imagery of John the Baptist shouting in the wilderness, bringing crowds of people to the Jordan River, and pouring water over them for the forgiveness of sin. But do you realize what he's saying? In Jerusalem, there was a watertight system for getting into the Temple and getting sins forgiven, for getting worthy, for declaring who's in and who's out. Now, they had this joker out in the desert, saying God is just as available *as water* and "God can raise up children of Abraham from these very stones" (see Matthew 3:9). No wonder the religious establishment wanted him dead! (We'll take a closer look at John in chapter six of this book.)

It is significant that Jesus went out to be baptized by John. Jesus is accepting the new world order to which John the Baptist is pointing. "Yes," he says, "God is as available as water in the river."

A Look from the Bottom

The historian Thomas F. Carney wrote in *The Shape of the Past: Models and Antiquity*: "The voices that speak to us from antiquity are overwhelmingly those of the cultured few, the elites. The modern voices that carry on their tale are overwhelmingly those of white, middle-class, European and North American males."[14] That is true: Most of the history we have is from less than 2 percent of the human population. Ninety-eight percent of the people who ever lived on this planet have been poor and uneducated.

Poor people didn't have the luxury to write their history, to tell us what it was like to be persecuted, oppressed, or simply forced to build a pyramid. We hear about pyramid building from the side of the pharaohs who planned the pyramids—not the hundreds of thousands of people who had to give their lives to build them.

We've missed most of the story of history. That's a new insight for many people in the modern age. Yet there are some exceptions, and the Bible is one of them. It's exciting to consider that the Bible is resistance literature. With the exception of Leviticus and Numbers, which were written by the priestly classes, most of the Bible was written by or about people who were occupied, enslaved, poor, or disenfranchised in some way.

In the Bible, we have a narrative from the bottom instead of from the top. Furthermore, it endured, which is remarkable when we consider that few of the books in the Bible were initially written down, but rather handed on orally. Besides, who wants to hear about life from the side of a slave, a woman, or a poor person? Even the Christian Scriptures reveal this residual bias when they end the multiplication stories with the telling phrase, "to say nothing of women and children" (Matthew 14:21). Exactly. "The scholarship of antiquity is often removed from the real world," continues Carney, "hygienically free of value judgments."[15]

The same is true in America today. Every year, we observe the Fourth of July and celebrate the heart-fluttering mythology that our founders loved freedom. Yet today we must acknowledge what they really meant when they said all "men" are created equal. The Declaration of Independence was written by rich white male landowners and it was addressing the enfranchisement of rich white males. The mythologies of private property, guns and violence, racism, and sexism are enshrined in the very foundation of the country.

American schoolchildren could easily get the idea that Jefferson's Declaration was a revolutionary document that empowered everyone to vote. Yet women weren't allowed to vote, and certainly Blacks were not; they weren't even counted as full persons in the census. The lie was that we *believed* that we believed all people were created equal! What made us think we were this great free society? Those at the top believed it then, and we at the top believe it two hundred years later. That's the power of myth.

The Diversity of Human Experience

Where I live in New Mexico, pilgrimages and images are more popular than sermons. Religion must express itself with music, dance, and art. Western Christianity has probably been very limited because it has been run mostly by an educated clergy. Yet many will not be led to God by a sermon or a book, by well-formulated theology, or even by logic.

This doesn't mean that some people are less smart, only that they come to reality in a different way, by intuitive leaps. My own father, for example, was a Kansas farmer. When he and Mom used to come and listen to me talk, my mother would just sit there, absorbed in my words, as many mothers might be. But Dad would fall asleep about ten minutes into it. Yet he didn't want to sleep through my talk, so he'd wake up and ask Mother, "Where does he get all those ideas?" In effect, he was saying, "Why do we need all those ideas?" Perhaps he was right.

If you're not a big idea person, trust that your way of naming reality works and is fine.

Native Americans in New Mexico dance, for example. Their dance has been their prayer. Then Christians came along and said, "Dance is secular." Yet why would someone giving their thoughts to God please God more than giving their body to God? It's just that many of us are biased in favor of the mind, thinking the mind is the supreme faculty.

That's not necessarily so! It's the bias of the elite, who often are overeducated in the head. Body, heart, and gut people come to God in different ways than through "correct" or interesting ideas.

My point here is that the Gospel is not primarily a set of facts, but *a way of seeing and a way of being in the world because of God*. Jesus speaks to the heart, saying, (1) God is on your side; (2) God can be trusted; (3) the universe is safe and benevolent; (4) trust yourselves, one another, and God; (5) there is no reason to be afraid; and (6) it's all heading toward something good. He does this primarily by touch, relationship, healing, and parables.

Jesus Is Pro-Feminine

In the Gospels, Jesus goes out of his way to honor the feminine viewpoint. In fact, he represents it in much of his own life. This is why most feminists don't criticize Jesus; they criticize Christianity—and rightly so! Jesus, in terms of sexism, is a man well ahead of his time, and his attitude is so out-of-culture that we could almost use it as an argument for his divine Sonship.

In the story of the woman at the well (John 4:1–42), for example, Jesus breaks all sorts of taboos by talking to a woman in public. By giving her credence, letting her talk back to him, and ignoring his disciples' discomfort, he violates the established codes of conduct. He knows those codes have no meaning in light of eternal values. Once Jesus touches on eternal values, he lets go of relative cultural values. He knows that they do not bind him.

The one story where it might seem that Jesus is dismissive and derogatory toward a pagan woman, telling her it is not fair to toss the children's (Israel's) food to the dogs (see Mark 7:24–30 or Matthew 15:21–28), turns out to be exactly the opposite. He initially seems to reflect the cultural, male, or religious prejudice toward her, but then accepts her rejoinder, admits he is wrong, praises her—and apologizes by healing her daughter! This is a perfect morality play of prejudice and patriarchy *overcome*.

Jesus truly was dangerous: He was creating a following with a kind of thinking that was much more on the side of inclusiveness than exclusiveness. That tension between exclusiveness and inclusiveness is one of the central themes of Jesus' ministry.

Jesus is always moving the boundaries outward while still respecting the center. That's the key to wisdom: being grounded in the center and still, from that deep foundation, knowing how to move out. The Greek Archimedes (c. 287–c. 212 BCE) declared, "Give me a lever and a place to stand and I can move the world." What Jesus had—and what we need—is a place to stand. The ground on which he stood was his experience of God. His lever was what we call the Gospel.

The danger of postmodern liberal society is that most people have no place to stand. Postmodern life is like a movable feast (or famine!): Everything is relative, in question, and in constant motion. Jesus gives his followers a clear place to stand—the tradition of Judaism—but he reinterprets the tradition. He moves the boundaries out from a stable and secure center.

Changing the Boundaries

We will see in the teaching of Jesus, and his Sermon on the Mount in particular, that he critiques and reorders the values of his culture from the bottom up. He "betrays" the prevailing institutions of family, religion, power, and resource control by his loyalty to another world vision, which he calls the Reign of God. Such loyalty cost him general popularity, the support of the authorities, immense inner agony, and finally his own life. By putting the picture in the largest possible frame, he called into question all smaller frames and forced a radical transformation of consciousness upon his hearers. Many were not ready for it.

In Jesus' world of the first century, the dominant institution was the kinship system: the family, the private home. That's why first-century Christian churches were house churches. They were nothing like what we might call our parish. Imagine small gatherings in private homes.

In Matthew's Gospel, the word *house* is used many times. Jesus is always going in and out of houses. And, like today, what happened around the tables in those houses both shaped and named the social order. That is the key to understanding the power Jesus exercised at table. That might be Jesus' most significant social demonstration: a social action with subversive consequences. The power and meaning of table fellowship in Jesus' life probably is why the Eucharist remained, especially in the Catholic tradition, as the central symbol. The Eucharist builds upon Jesus' tradition of eating in a new way. We'll examine that more closely in the next chapter of this book.

Economics and the Western World

In our social setup, family isn't first—as we are becoming painfully aware—nor is religion, nor even politics. What drives the institutions (government, social policy, and the like) in our culture is *money*. Some people say politics is the driving institution, but people often are politically naïve, ignorant of the underlying power and reality of the economy.

The dominant institution in our society is the system of production and consumption. The central value of our culture is buying and selling. It pervades everything. Advertisements appear on every screen. Commercialism has invaded everything because the entire system is built on the commandments "Thou shalt produce" and "Thou shalt consume."

Sometimes I turn on the TV talk shows when I'm reading my mail. It's a window into how Middle America thinks. One show featured "freeloaders"—people who live off their grandmother or another family member or friend. The wrath from the studio audience toward these people was uncanny! It was not just that they were taking advantage of someone's generosity. It was as if the freeloaders had broken the ultimate taboo: They were not producers. Several of them said they live on almost nothing and that's why they can do it. That meant they were breaking a double taboo: They weren't consuming either!

I'll bet we've all heard friends talk as if being a consumer is a religious act. How did we turn reality around to make consumption a virtue? If we listen to people's conversations, we can hear it: "I bought a new car, even though my old one worked fine. It's good for the economy." It could only happen in a culture where economics is the number one institution and the other three (family, religion, and politics) are subservient to it.

The form of authority in America is not patriarchy, as it would be in most kinship societies. (That probably explains some of our problem with priesthood and the papacy.) The father figure once symbolically held the family together, but that is changing as "family" is defined much more broadly. Authority is not religious ideology, as in a religious culture, or party authority, as in a political culture. Quite simply, it is wealth. Status in our society is attained by having money and the freedom to use it.

Religion in an Economic Culture

There have been cultures where religious authority dominated. Medieval European Christendom agreed upon giving primary meaning to God and the Christian religion. That doesn't mean they fully lived it out or that all the structures were Christian, but there was an agreed-upon meaning system. Today, we have the same in the Islamic states, and it's scaring Westerners to death. Religion as the primary institution has more power to gather people than anything else because religion speaks to the depth of the soul. Islam is again a force to be reckoned with in the world because it still has what Christianity once had in the twelfth century: the culture held together by the power of the image of God.

When the economic institution is our primary lens, religion tends to be diluted by pragmatic, win/lose, and power attitudes. God is bought and sold more than waited for, surrendered to, or loved. Those of us from economic cultures need to meditate hard and long about why Jesus' one clear act of anger was aimed at those selling and buying in the Temple (see Matthew 21:12).

I once saw a cartoon in *The New Yorker* depicting a pedestal with a dollar bill enthroned on it. All the people around are bowing down. One person who is bowing down says, "The reason I like this religion is that at least we're not hypocritical." We Americans have this dangerous illusion that we're a religious people. Yet it's evident to anybody who pays attention that God is not on the pedestal here. Clearly, our consumer system is on the pedestal and everything else is subservient: Market morality, the marketing of politicians, and families are all revolving around mass consumption.

I once was teaching a class that was to be attended by a recently converted wealthy banker. I had been warned that he probably would take me to task for my criticism of the American Way, so I was prepared for the worst. I watched him during my talk: the man in the three-piece suit, listening attentively, occasionally becoming stiff-shouldered. And sure enough, at break time, he headed right for my podium.

"Here it comes," I thought, "the lecture on the 'bottom line' that I hear from time to time from upset businessmen."

"Father," he said, putting his hands on my shoulders, "I've got something to tell you. Not only is what you said true, but it's much truer than you even imagine." He then explained to me a study that documented that the United States government's savings and loan bailout of 1989 was the biggest transfer of money from the poor to the rich in human history.

"But there's really no one to blame," he added, "in spite of the visible few who went to jail for their corrupt actions. The whole system is skewed to protect those at the top at all costs."

In fact, it's to protect the system itself, because the system is our goal. We abhor and denigrate welfare for the poor, but hardly blink at welfare for corporations or for the banking and military systems.

Those of us who were working in social service agencies before the Persian Gulf War will remember how tight money was for education programs, health care, libraries, or almost any social institution. Washington always said they were out of money—even money for infrastructure, like rebuilding bridges. These were called "special interests." Then, suddenly, we had billions of dollars to fight the Persian Gulf War to protect our access to oil and wealthy Kuwait. How did we get money overnight? Because it's always there to protect the system itself. That *is* the system: militarism and money. These are not "special interests" in an economic culture; they are prevailing common interest.

Honor and Shame: Then and Now

In a kinship society like Jesus', status was achieved through the honor/shame system. Therein lies the key to many of Jesus' examples. In the honor/shame system, someone gains status, self-image, and meaning primarily through how others see them. The system around Jesus didn't ask the individual to think in terms of "who I really am before God" (as Jesus did), or "what I feel about myself" (modern American culture), but rather, "How does my village see me?" Tribal cultures, to this day, are built on some kind of honor/shame system. That's how most societies operated before they became highly urbanized and industrialized. Our meaning was almost entirely tied up in how our family and friends saw us. It gave great comfort to the ego, and it also gave great power for social control.

Japan is a modern example of a kinship system, where the old honor/shame system still operates (although it has begun changing to an economic system). Once when I was preaching in Japan, I had with me two young men from the New Jerusalem Community (of which I was pastor in the 1970s), whom we'd sent to work with the poor in the Philippines. These two missionaries had expensive cameras with them when we stopped to see the Hiroshima Peace Memorial Museum. Yet a sign said cameras were prohibited. The Japanese man who was showing us around said, "Just leave them here on the curb and we'll pick them up when we get back out."

There were thousands of people walking by in all directions. My two friends were understandably anxious, but our guide assured us the cameras would be untouched. "We just don't steal, you know." Then he said that if the cameras were stolen, he'd buy them new ones. They left their two expensive cameras on the curb at Hiroshima and we went into the museum. We walked all the way through. When we got up to the second floor, my friend Michael looked out the window and there the cameras were, with Japanese walking all around them. An hour and a half later, we returned to find the cameras untouched. It made me wonder why some call the United States a Christian nation and think of the Japanese as "pagans." The honor/shame system is largely gone for us. It is a stronger enforcer of morals than mere religious commandments.

It should be obvious: For new wine, we will have to have new wineskins. Until we have new wineskins—a new social order—it doesn't make a bit of difference to teach people "Thou shalt not steal" and "Thou shalt not be greedy." Our system is set up on the assumption that greed at the top will "trickle down" to the poor on the bottom. President Ronald Reagan was the first one to put it so bluntly, but that's been the system all along. It doesn't change much from one leader to the next. The Gospel gives us the ability to stand outside of our own institutions and to see them with clarity.

In Jesus' time, shame and honor were in fact moral values that people felt compelled to follow. If a situation called for retaliation, you had to retaliate. Not to retaliate would have been immoral, because you would have abandoned your honor. You were bound to be true to the honor of your village, your family, yourself. For Jesus to walk into the midst of that and say, "Do not retaliate" was to subvert the whole honor/shame system.

Once challenged, Jesus' listeners were given a new place to find their identity: in God. Who we are in God is who we are. That's the end of ups and downs. My value no longer depends upon whether my family or village likes me, whether I'm good-looking, wealthy, or obedient to the laws. Jesus' message is incredibly subversive in an honor/shame society! Yet, as he takes away their old foundations, he offers a new, more solid one: neither shame- nor guilt-based, but based in who we are in God.

Saint Francis said the same thing to his society: Who I am is who I am in God, nothing more, nothing less. Although that might sound scary at first, it actually is good news. Who we are in God is a beloved daughter or a beloved son; we are no longer dependent on our culture's estimation, or even our own. Through our prayer, our awareness of God within us, we continually discover our true identity: "The life you have is hidden with Christ in God" (Colossians 3:3b).

Honor is the opposite of what prayer teaches the heart. It is the value of a person in our own eyes, or through the eyes of others. Honor is excellence as recognized by society, and therefore self-image and human value are forever shaky, changing, and unreliable. To counter such externalization, Jesus promotes the three religious disciplines found in all the great world religions: prayer, almsgiving, and fasting. These are the three time-tested ways to get free from the false self. Yet Jesus adds a twist: In all three cases, he says, do it secretly. Why? Because by doing these practices away from others' eyes, we break our enmeshment in other people's image of us. We find our identity within ourselves and in a transcendent reference point.

I am glad we coined the word *codependency*. Even if we overuse the term, we've named why most people don't have a very solid self-image. For some, it's entirely based on what their spouse thinks of them—and when their spouse dies, they die. It's almost as if their narrative is, "I'm no one apart from what my husband, wife, children, or others think of me"—which must be monitored, assessed, and controlled, day by day. What basic insecurity for people living in the modern world!

Without the spiritual journey, we're all enmeshed, even if we're not in a kinship-based society. Without the contemplative journey into true self, we are who our neighbor says we are. We fall deeper into this fragile self as we preoccupy ourselves with celebrities, soap operas, and the cults of public figures. Infotainment takes the place of documentary. Images take the place of substance.

How many can live up to society's standards of worth: good looking, blonde, slim, making money, a jetsetter? Surely no more than 5 percent of people can live up to these images. All the rest of us, in some way, feel inadequate, stupid, and ugly. That's why teen suicide is at an all-time high, why every social indicator reveals that we are a massively deteriorating culture. Our cultural standards for success are narrower than religion's standards ever were, and the result is widespread feelings of inadequacy.

This is an issue for both women and men in our culture. Women, especially, are expected to live up to an impossible ideal in terms of youthful looks, slim figures, body proportions. It can be an uphill struggle to maintain self-esteem if you don't fit the mold. Men, too, tend to define their worth in terms of outside factors like appearance, power, and job status. Economic cultures tend to produce more and more men who are unacceptable and outsiders to the system of success. No wonder that America continues to hold the record for the highest per-capita incarceration rate in the world.[16]

When I spent time in hermitage, I would face this at a level that surprised me. I was ashamed to admit it to myself. When I got away from the crowds, who always listen to my preaching and feed my ego, I was at a bit of a loss. At a really deep level, I felt a fear of insignificance, of being nothing. When I saw that within myself, I wept. I saw me trying to prove myself, somehow, over the years, and finding my self-worth in my success as an evangelist. I saw within myself a false motive for much of my work—and I was ashamed before God because of what I saw.

Yet, I think that motive of proving ourselves is in all of us. Each of us carries that terrible fear that we are nothing: "Among the almost eight billion of us on this planet, how could God notice me?"

Every town has the hard-to-get-to spot where the teens paint graffiti, late at night, at tremendous risk. Yet, when the soul feels utterly insignificant, it writes its name where we can't miss it. I once visited our lay missionaries from the New Jerusalem Community who were working in Saint Lucia, a little island in the Caribbean. A student at a local high school said to me, "Father, do you know that our island isn't even on some maps of the world?" And we think we feel insignificant! Almost everyone there is too poor to ever move anywhere else. Imagine if your little dot, the only world you'll ever know, isn't even on the map.

Without God, without being tied to the eternal, the soul collapses into insignificance. The tendency is to hand over our momentary significance to other people's estimation of us. That's an honor/shame society. Do you see the genius of advising such folks to pray, fast, and give alms *in secret*? Jesus calls them to interiority, to find their validation in God alone.

Only prayer lets you realize that who you are is who you were in God before anybody thought anything: before you thought about whether you are good or bad, before anybody else thought about whether you are good or bad. You came forth from God and you will return to God. You are eternal. That's the only solid ground. That's the rock of the spiritual journey. That's what Jesus means when he says in Luke's Gospel that "your names are written in heaven" (10:20b). You're an eternal creation of God and there's no point in denying it or trying to dress it up; it already is. That's the ultimate good news.

But the good side of an honor/shame system is that it makes communities much more possible. It creates a world of interdependent people who rely upon one another, who stick together, who understand loyalty and commitment. We don't have that anymore because we're all largely trying to define ourselves through media images that are not connected with our identification as brother, sister, or family. Thus, we see community collapsing. It's very hard to create community or cooperation in such a world. That's a difference between our times and Jesus' times: Jesus preached in a world where community was still understood, where an appropriate sense of honor and shame kept people bound and loyal to their commitments and to one another.

We live in a world where honor and shame are merely manipulated, month by month and moment by moment, through TV, tabloids, social media, commercials, and even the marketing of politics and court cases. It seems like every few months the moral issue about which we should feel shame or outrage changes: sexual harassment, crime, teen pregnancy, pedophilia, the deficit, family violence, abortion, racial injustice, and so on. We cannot build a community of values unless we are a part of something more solid and enduring—where appropriate honor and shame reflect perennial human qualities to which we are locally accountable.

As we will see in the next chapter, the meal became Jesus' model for such teaching.

chapter five

Table Fellowship in the Christian Scriptures

Jesus didn't want his community to have a social ethic; he wanted it to *be* a social ethic. Their very way of relating was to be an affront to the system of dominance and power; it was to name reality in a new way. They were to live in a new symbolic universe. This radical idea is given in a simple clue found throughout the Christian Scriptures—one biblical scholars overlooked until only recently: Jesus' presence with others at table. That theme is so constant in the Christian Scriptures that scholars today see it as central to Jesus' message.

I'm no scholar, but I have a tremendous respect for what scholars do. After wading through the footnotes of a number of studies on the historical Jesus, I hope to be able to share in plain language what I've discovered. You may be as surprised as I was that we didn't see it all along.

In *The Historical Jesus*, Christian Scriptures scholar John Dominic Crossan writes of Jesus: "He tells the missionaries not to carry a bag because they do not beg for alms or food or clothing or anything else and they do not carry bread. They share a miracle and a kingdom and they receive in return a table and a house."[17]

Here, I think, is the heart of the original "Jesus Movement." That's an expression the scholars use and I think it's a good one. Calling the original gathering the Jesus Movement helps us avoid getting concerned with church language too early. We need to understand the Jesus Movement before we can understand its later evolution into a church, as noted in these quotes by Crossan and anthropologist Gillian Feeley-Harnik.

[There is] a shared egalitarianism of spiritual (healing) and material (eating) resources [among Jesus' followers]. I emphasize this
as strongly as possible, and I maintain that its materiality and
spirituality, its facticity and symbolism, cannot be separated. The
mission we are talking about is not, like Paul's, a dramatic thrust
along major trade routes to urban centers hundreds of miles
apart. Yet it concerns the longest journey in the Greco-Roman
world, maybe in any world—the step across the threshold of a
peasant stranger's home.[18]

Shared home and common meal must be understood against
the cross-cultural anthology of food and commensalism [table
fellowship]. It is owing precisely to the complex interaction of
cultural categories that food is commonly one of the principal
ways in which differences among social groups are marked.[19]

Crossan goes on to describe an anthropologist's research of many studies,
with the conclusion that in all cultures, sharing food is a complex interaction that symbolizes group relationships and defines group boundaries
almost more than any other daily event.

We have no doubt become more aware of this if we've ever spent any
time away from home with a group of new acquaintances. We experienced it constantly at our guest house for work interns at the Center
for Action and Contemplation in New Mexico. Groups of interns would
come and live in our guest house for months at a time. Over the years,
there was probably no single issue that brought up more feelings and
discussion than food. A tremendous amount of time is put into what we
buy, how much we pay for it, who gets it, who fixes it, how much is fixed,
with what quality, and who cleans up afterward.

There is tremendous symbolism connected to food. That we eat this
and don't eat that means something. Certain kinds of people eat certain
kinds of food. Through our choices and behavior at table, we name and
identify ourselves. For example, a vegetarian diet has been a conscious

choice for some because they've studied the politics of food: who eats meat and who can't eat meat; what eating meat is doing, not only to our health, but even to the planet.

Other scholars continue the theme: "Food exchanges are able to act as symbols of human interaction. Eating is a behavior which symbolizes feelings and relationships, mediates social status and power, expresses the boundaries of group identity."[20]

Whom you eat with defines whom you *don't* eat with. During the years I was pastor of New Jerusalem Community in Cincinnati, that was really hard for me. There was one of me and as many as three hundred New Jerusalem community members. It was more symbolic than I ever wanted it to be when I would accept an invitation to somebody's house for supper. If I went to one family's house, I worried that others would be jealous. Eventually, I found myself avoiding those invitations and limiting myself to communal or social obligations.

Jesus never appears to be pushing what we call social programs as such. He is much more radical. He is calling us to a new social order where we literally share table differently. Dorothy Day was apparently right on target when she founded houses of hospitality as her primary message of evangelization. The poor are welcomed to the table. Remember Jesus' instructions to the missionaries: The disciples are to go out with no money or traveling bag, or footwear (see Matthew 10:10). They are to be in need of hospitality and enter into other people's worlds and mercy.

My father Francis took this very literally. That kept the early Franciscans on the move so we couldn't become an establishment and force the people to come to us. Francis went out into the world of the poor, entering into it on their terms. Can you imagine if we had taken Jesus' commands to the missionaries seriously, how different the evangelization of Mexico would have been? What if we had not brought along all our European baggage to the evangelization of the New World?

Indeed, those Gospel instructions are the only directives Jesus gave us. He didn't tell missionaries to teach the Creed or the Trinity. He simply said, "Don't take any traveling bag, don't take any money in your belt." That's why Francis wore a rope: A belt was a wallet and he wanted to show he didn't have any money. He was totally dependent upon the poor; he had to enter into their world. What extraordinary symbolism! Both Jesus and Francis entered into others' worlds and let them invite the disciples as their house guests. In that way grace, life, could be poured back and forth. How beautiful! It has the ring of truth. Many missionaries are rediscovering it today.

Consider your own relationships with those who invite you over to eat at their home. Sharing table fellowship repeatedly builds a history of trust. To build that trust is as simple as entering into their house and accepting hospitality. That kind of trust has taken me through some hard times with friends—times when others turned against me. The people with whom I ate were willing to stand beside me even when they didn't understand what I was going through. We had sat side-by-side as equals around a table. I had come into their world, without society's pretenses, as their friend and confidant. Eating together in one another's homes radically changes the nature of social relationship, much more than we might have thought.

The mystery of sharing food and a common table takes place on different levels. First, there is the unifying idea of sharing the same food. Then there is the whole symbolism of the table itself: where you sit at the table, how the table is arranged. Together, the food and table become a symbol of how our social world is arranged. Once we rearrange life around the table, we begin to change our notions of social life.

That, I believe, was Jesus' most consistent social action: eating in new ways. In the midst of that eating, he announced the Reign of God and spoke in new ways. Usually, on his way in or out of the house, he encountered those who were oppressed and eliminated from the system. A great number of Jesus' healings and exorcisms take place while he's either entering a house to have a meal with someone or leaving a house after just having had a meal with someone. He redefines where power is on many different levels at the same time. Religious power is, for one thing, mostly exercised outside the Temple and synagogue.

It is necessary to calculate very carefully what was lost and what was gained as Christianity developed. The church moved from Jesus' real meal with open table fellowship to the relatively safe ritual meal that became the Christian Eucharist.

Unfortunately, the meal itself came to redefine social reality in a negative way, in terms of worthiness and unworthiness. That is almost exactly the opposite of Jesus' intention. To this day, we use Eucharist to define membership in terms of who is worthy and unworthy. Even if we deny that is our intention, it is clearly the practical message that people hear. We must ask whether people work out relationships independently and then come over for supper (sometimes), or if the invitation to come over for supper is not the healing way to work out the relationship.

Second, it is strange and inconsistent that sins of marriage and sexuality seem to be the only ones that exclude people from the table, even when other sins like greed and hatefulness are more of a public scandal.

Of what is Jesus accused by his contemporaries? By one side, he is accused of eating with tax collectors and sinners (Matthew 9:10–11, for example); and by the other side, of eating too much (Luke 7:34), or eating with the Pharisees and lawyers (Luke 7:36–50, 11:37–54, 14:1). He ate with both sides. He ate with lepers (Mark 14:3), received a woman with a bad reputation at a men's dinner (Luke 7:36–37), and even invited himself over to a "sinner's" house (Luke 19:1–10). He didn't please anybody, it seems—always breaking the rules and expanding the table.

A Universal Table

But don't take just the scholars' word for it. Let's examine the Christian Scriptures themselves. The most powerful examples are in Mark and

Luke. Why not Matthew? Because Matthew's Gospel is addressed to a first-century equivalent of the middle class. Matthew, for example, takes "How blessed are you who are poor" (Luke 6:20b) and softens it a bit into "How blessed are the poor in spirit" (Matthew 5:3a). He's trying to prevent his "middle class" audience from writing him off at the outset. The open table fellowship is very often weakened in Matthew's Gospel, compared to Mark and Luke. Mark and Luke are the harder, more challenging Gospels.

In light of that softness, Matthew's Gospel is probably well suited for most of us. Middle-class people can hear Matthew more quickly than they can hear Luke. Luke is talking to the poor in a way that will make them feel invited and accepted by God. Mark is doing the same thing for people with a little more security, it seems. This is a good example of how we should speak in a way that enables us to be heard. (Paul is a master at this, and proud of it; see 1 Corinthians 9:19–23.)

Luke 14 is one of the most powerful passages. In the first sentence of that chapter, there are two shocking things we probably miss on Sunday because they come at the very beginning of the reading. (We're barely settled into our seats and the first sentence is over already!) "Now, it happened that on a Sabbath day he had gone to share a meal in the house of one of the leading Pharisees" (14:1a). That sets the stage: Jesus is entering totally into the world of the establishment on a highly regulated day, a day when all good Jews should do certain things and should not do other things.

Jesus is in place to break all kinds of rules and to upset lots of people. He's eating with the cultural and religious establishment, the leading Pharisees. That, in itself, is undoubtedly upsetting the social activists in town, the liberals. Can't you hear them: "What is he doing going over and eating in the Northeast Heights with the rich people?!"

The verse concludes, "and they watched him closely" (14:1b). These are the passive-aggressive types. They appear to be his friends, but they're just waiting for him to slip up. It's very hard to win in such situations, as you know. They want to see what this man is really about: "We'll invite him to our house and see what he's up to."

"Now there in front of him was a man with dropsy"—we're not told how this man got in—"and Jesus addressed the lawyers and Pharisees with the words, 'Is it against the law to cure someone on the Sabbath, or not?' But they remained silent" (14:2–4a). The pernicious nature of passive-aggressive people is that they maintain a positive self-image while, on another level, wishing or intending ill. It's also one of those cases where they knew, no matter what they answered, they'd displease someone, so they kept their mouths shut.

"So he took the man and cured him and sent him away. Then he said to them"—he knows they're upset, he knows they're trying to get him, so he challenges them—"'Which of you here, if his son falls into a well, or his ox, will not pull him out on a Sabbath day without any hesitation?' And to this they could find no answer" (14:5b–6).

This first example is fundamental. The law at this period of Jewish history is being interpreted almost exclusively through the Book of Leviticus, particularly chapters 17–24, the Law of Holiness. That interpretation is characterized by: (1) obeying the law literally, (2) ritual observance of cult, and (3) keeping one's group and group symbols pure. Holiness is thought of as a separatist purity. Such an emphasis continually reemerges in right-wing movements in every age: correct code, cult, and community.

Issues of exclusion and inclusion are absolutely central to the Law of Holiness. This is what Jesus takes on, front and center: his own tradition from the Torah. He refuses to interpret the Mosaic law in terms of the Leviticus Law of Holiness, in terms of inclusion/exclusion, the symbolic self-identification of Judaism as the righteous, pure, elite group.

Jesus continually interprets the Law of Holiness in terms of the God whom he has met—and that God is always about *compassion* and *mercy*.

Harvard psychologist Lawrence Kohlberg (1927–1987) described six stages in human moral development, starting from infancy. Jesus is the person at Kohlberg's sixth level of morality (enlightenment or universal ethical principles), largely preaching to people at levels two and three (selfish need and peer pressure), and an institution that doesn't want people who go beyond level four and a half (socially defined roles for the common good), because then they won't idolize the institution anymore.

When the law gets in the way of human compassion, Jesus simply disregards the law. He has found its *meaning*. As he says most clearly about picking and eating grain on the sabbath (see Mark 2:23–28), the law is not an end in itself. It's a means to an end. The law was made for humanity; humanity was not made for the law, Jesus says (see Mark 2:27).

That's cataclysmic. It undercuts most of institutional religion since the beginning of time. Religion tends to idolize law, to make group boundaries and the symbols of the group ends in themselves. At that point, Jesus departs from what would become rabbinic Judaism and sets out on a path that eventually would become Christianity. (Although the same pattern will be repeated there, as it always is in every life.)

Surely that is not the way he thought about it, though. When dying on the cross, in his human mind, he must have fully thought of himself as a good Jewish man, not the founder of Christianity (much less the Roman Catholic Church, United Methodist Church, or any other church). We don't want to hear that, but that's who Jesus was: a good Jew trying to reform Judaism in terms of moving the boundaries outward. As one who has tasted God's infinite love, he has a vision that defies society's boundaries.

He moves them out so much that Paul then goes out and invites the gentiles in. Peter (and those closest to him) wasn't ready for that, as we see in Acts 11:1–18 and Galatians 2. Yet Jesus created the possibility of a universal religion for all nations. He was not the kind of Messiah that Judaism expected, or even wanted.

The reason Christianity has the power to be a universal religion is precisely because of this doctrine of open table fellowship—which the other monotheistic religions do not teach so clearly, except at the mystical level. For us, it should be first-level teaching. If only people who rightly accept Jesus as their "exclusive savior" would also accept his teaching of utter *inclusivity*! Too often, we seem to worship the messenger almost as an avoidance of the message. The ego will use any subterfuge to remain in control.

Now, let's get back to Jesus' dinner conversation with the leading Pharisees in Luke 14.

> He then told the guests a parable, because he had noticed how they picked the places of honor. He said this, "When someone invites you to a wedding feast, do not take your seat in the place of honor. A more distinguished person than you may have been invited, and the person who invited you both may come and say, 'Give up your place to this man.' And then, to your embarrassment, you will have to go and take the lowest place. No; when you are a guest, *make your way to the lowest place and sit there*, so that, when your host comes, he may say, 'My friend, move up higher.' Then, everyone with you at the table will see you honored...."
>
> Then he said to his host, "When you give a lunch or a dinner, do not invite your friends or your brothers or your relations or rich neighbors, in case they invite you back and so repay you. No; when you have a party, invite the poor, the crippled, the lame, the blind; *then you will be blessed, for they have no means to repay you* and so you will be repaid when the upright rise again."
>
> On hearing this, one of those gathered round the table said to him, "Blessed is anyone who will share the meal in the kingdom of God!" (Luke 14:7–10, 12–15, emphases added)

The table in the Reign of God is one where, first of all, insiders are not seeking status. It's a table that does not honor class, but in fact prefers what Matthew finally calls the least of the brothers and sisters: the crippled, the lame and the blind, the outsiders. In his description of banquet tables, Jesus undercuts all meritocracy and proclaims "blessed" those who opt out of the game or those excluded from society.

What follows in Luke 14:15–24 is a third banquet parable, the one where the invited guests all offer excuses for not coming to a wedding feast. Notice that these are *good* excuses; these are not bad people. One had bought a piece of land, another had bought five oxen that required his attention, the third is a newlywed. These are nice, proper folks doing appropriate things. (The call to the Gospel life is not really a call to be moral, law-abiding, and "good," although many seem to think so. It is, rather, *to follow Jesus*—who keeps us on the path of letting go and rediscovering, which is very different from just "being good." Think about that!)

Historians claim that the law may never have been more carefully observed than during this period of Jewish history. The Jews of Jesus' day, including those who played a part in Jesus' death, were not bad people! What killed Jesus was not bad people; it was *good people following conventional wisdom*. Unless we understand that, the essential conflict of the Gospels will never hit us. Those who rejected Jesus were doing all the right things. They were nice Jewish citizens who had not yet heard about the Reign of God.

If you forget the rest of this book, please remember just this: Religion is all the things you normally go through to meet God. The Gospel is the way you will see and think *after* you have met God. The Gospel is the effect of the God-encounter. Religion, though it often stirs desire, is also the most common and disguised way of *avoiding* the encounter. The parable ends on an ominous note: "Not one of those who were invited shall have a taste of my banquet" (Luke 14:24). Religion is the invitation; the Gospel is the banquet.

Eating with Sinners

Jesus' "Code of Compassion" is found in Mark (2:13–15) as well:

> He went out again to the shore of the lake; and all the people came to him, and he taught them. As he was walking along, he saw Levi, the son of Alphaeus, sitting at the tax office, and he said to him, "Follow me." And he got up and followed him.
>
> When Jesus was at dinner in his house, a number of tax collectors and sinners were also sitting at table with Jesus and his disciples; *for there were many of them among his followers.* (emphasis added)

Apparently, this Levi is a tax collector, one of the people who were stealing from the poor and pocketing plenty of money. Jesus calls Levi from this group, who are the oppressors, and goes immediately to eat at his house. By going there, he is already moving his disciples beyond their comfort zone. It is easy to imagine Simon the Zealot and Judas remaining outside, grumbling.

The word *sinners* usually conjures up for us notions of judgment and morality. In Jesus' day, sinners were clearly defined by the Levitical Law of Holiness. That definition is not the same as today, at least on the surface. In those days, you were either a sinner or not a sinner, and everybody knew which one you were. If you were not able to follow the purification rules, the debt codes, and the purity codes, you knew you were a sinner, and others did too. It was an objective category more than a subjective accusation.

These codes, ironically, created more and more sinners. In Jesus' day, there was an increasing emphasis on the codes. You had to jump through the hoops at the Temple and pay money to jump through each hoop. Thus, more and more people couldn't afford *not* to be sinners, because their location, job, or money kept them from ritual observance. Shepherds were in this category, for example, which might enlighten your reading of the Christmas story.

"How horrible those times were!" you might say. Yet, in today's society, we do much the same thing. We wouldn't openly give such a moral tinge to poverty, but our society still looks down on the people who can't pay their way. Consider the shameful way people talk about welfare recipients. In the Gospels, wherever you read "sinners," it simply refers to the people who can't do it right—very often because they can't afford the Temple fees. It might drive the point home for modern Americans, when reading these passages, to replace "sinners" with "people on welfare" or "unemployed," "uneducated," "homeless," "in jail"—the effect is the same.

Back to our story: "When the scribes of the Pharisee party saw him eating with sinners and tax collectors, they said to his disciples, 'Why does he eat with tax collectors and sinners?'" (Mark 2:16).

Just when his good disciples were about to say, "I wish I knew!" Jesus said to them, "It is not the healthy who need the doctor, but the sick. I came to call not the upright, but sinners" (Mark 2:17b–c). Jesus does not see his task as gathering an elite of the "saved," but founding a general hospital for the throwaways.

It is easy for us to write off these scribes and Pharisees as self-righteous, arrogant people. But that is not the issue. They feel bound by the shame and honor codes that shape their lives. They're just doing what's expected. But Jesus isn't, so he challenges them. By eating with tax collectors and sinners—and accepting no shame—Jesus is discounting the only worldview they know. We would react the same way, I'm sure: with outrage and scandal!

This tension comes up anywhere Jesus confronts the rules that allowed the religious elite to feel more righteous than anyone else. In fasting, for example, Jesus observes that the elite would have a problem with him no matter what he did: They wouldn't listen to John, who wouldn't eat or drink, and now Jesus comes along, eating and drinking, and they don't like him either (see Matthew 11:18–19). It's obvious to Jesus they just don't want the truth. He says he would rather sin on the side of eating and drinking, which probably upsets them more.

Now let's look at this call of Matthew in Matthew's Gospel: "As Jesus was walking on from there, he saw a man named Matthew [who apparently is the same as Levi] sitting at the tax office, and he said to him, 'Follow me.' And he got up and followed him" (9:9).

The quick response of several of the disciples seems to name the quality Jesus desires—risk-takers over the security conscious. Anybody who has worked with personnel knows the difference.

The story continues, just as in Mark, but with a different interpretation. "Now, while he was at table in the house, it happened that a number of tax collectors and sinners came to sit at the table with Jesus and his disciples. When the Pharisees saw this, they said to his disciples, 'Why does your master eat with tax collectors and sinners?'" (9:10–11).

And Jesus repeats the same line as in Mark: "It is not the healthy who need the doctor, but the sick" (9:12). It seems to me that Jesus is saying *relationship* reality is above *ritual* reality. People are more important than ideology. Thus, we are to go where we're needed. We are to go where we're invited. We are to go where life is wanted and where it is received. "Go and learn the meaning of the words, 'Mercy is what pleases me, not sacrifice'" (Matthew 9:13a).

Undoubtedly, Jesus says this because in the desert he met a God of mercy and remembered this not-so-quoted line from Hosea: "For faithful love is what pleases me, not sacrifice; knowledge of God, not burnt offerings" (Hosea 6:6).

This is the God that Jesus called Father, Abba. It's not that Jesus is a liberal or one who thinks boundaries don't matter. No, he has met the God who is "mercy within mercy within mercy."[21]

Meeting that kind of God allows you to proclaim a Gospel of mercy, above and beyond the formulations of those who quote but do not know.

The authority of Jesus—unlike the good scribes—is that he *knows* for himself, and calls us to know for ourselves.

When I see political correctness on the left becoming just as rigid and righteous as patriotic correctness on the right, I know again that Jesus was very wise. The church, as Jesus seems to be defining it, is the gathering of accepted brokenness. It's *not* the gathering of the saved. (Matthew 9:13 is the final punch line: "And indeed I came to call not the upright, but sinners.")

The church is never a "members-only" club. Isn't it sad that the church became the gathering of the saved instead of what Jesus makes it in his open table of fellowship? Jesus' table is the gathering of the *un*saved! Sometimes fellow priests tell me, "We're preaching to the choir. We're saving the saved. We just keep gathering the same two hundred people to sing Jesus songs and read the Bible. And we convince one another that we're saved and that we're holy." That's what happens when the church becomes established in one place, when the people come to the church instead of us going to them. We create the congregation of the "enlightened"—who, by that very token, are not enlightened at all.

The message is clear: What we normally call morality is simply not what Jesus was into. Jesus redefines reality in terms of who God is—not little people's moral categories about what makes me good and you bad. The God encounter, of course, demands of us a much higher morality than creed, code, or cult ever would.

We see that Jesus gets very impatient with external religion when he goes to the house of a Pharisee. As I mentioned before, Jesus eats with the elite, but he always challenges them. He seems to have forgotten Miss Manners' rules for guests:

> A Pharisee invited him to dine at his house. He went in and sat down at table. The Pharisee saw this and was surprised that he had not first washed before the meal. But the Lord said to him, "You Pharisees! You clean the outside of cup and plate, while

inside yourselves you are filled with extortion and wickedness. Fools! Did not he who made the outside make the inside too?" (Luke 11:37b–40)

The point of the passage is this: Worry about the inner attitude instead of being preoccupied with the outer ritual. "You pay your tithe of mint and rue and all sorts of garden herbs and neglect justice and the love of God! These you should have practiced, without neglecting the others" (11:42b).

It's never either/or for Jesus; it's a matter of sequence, priority, and motivation. Get the center point clear and then the rituals are OK. Rituals are not to be idolized; they are only rituals.

But Jesus never throws them out, either (liberals, take heed!). People need to have a symbolic and celebrated universe. There is no healthy religion without metaphor, symbol, or ritual. Without some creed, code, and cult, a group will make no impact on the world or themselves as a community. The temptation today is to revert to private enlightenment with no accountability systems or community base.

In the rest of Luke 11, Jesus uses table fellowship to challenge the entire religious system. You'll see that his greatest challenges come with those who are thinking well of themselves. There is another strong example in Luke 7:36–50: "One of the Pharisees invited him to a meal. When he arrived at the Pharisee's house and took his place at table, suddenly a woman came in" (7:36–37a).

Now understand, it's men only at meals, just like the Greek "symposium," where great ideas and food were shared. That's the only world they know. A woman's place is in the kitchen—which is the whole meaning of the Martha/Mary story in Luke 10: Martha becomes upset when Mary leaves the kitchen. Women are in the outer rooms, just as they are in the outer courts of the Temple.

In this story, not only does this woman crash a male symposium and dinner party, but this woman had a bad name in town. She had heard Jesus was dining with the Pharisee and had brought with her an alabaster jar of ointment. She waited behind him at his feet, which is *behind* Jesus, because at a meal, the men all reclined on the floor, heads closest to the center, where they could have food and good conversation for hours on end.

> She waited behind him at his feet, weeping, and her tears fell on his feet, and she wiped them away with her hair; then she covered his feet with kisses and anointed them with the ointment. (Luke 7:38)

Anyone knows what a group of men would assume when they saw that. Imagine the snickering! Uncovered hair was surely not the symbol of an upright or attached woman. And she kisses him—and he lets her. What must this imply?! What happened between Jesus and this woman?

> When the Pharisee who had invited him saw this, he said to himself, "If this man were a prophet, he would know who this woman is and what sort of person it is who is touching him and what a bad name she has." Then Jesus said, "Simon, I have something to say to you." (Luke 7:39–40a)

Jesus never shames people. He just states the truth, which probably sometimes shames people, but that's not his intention.

> He replied, "Say on, Master."
>
> "There was once a creditor who had two men in his debt; one owed him five hundred denarii, the other fifty. They were unable to pay, so he let them both off. Which of them will love him more?"
>
> Simon answered, "The one who was let off more, I suppose."
>
> Jesus said, "You are right."
>
> Then he turned to the woman and said to Simon, "You see this woman? I came into your house, and you poured no water over my feet, but she has poured out her tears over my feet and

wiped them away with her hair. You gave me no kiss, but she has been covering my feet with kisses ever since I came in. You did not anoint my head with oil, but she has anointed my feet with ointment. For this reason, I tell you that *her sins, many as they are, have been forgiven her, because she has shown such great love.*" (Luke 7:41–47a, emphasis added)

That's a very interesting turn of phrase at the end. We would probably say a loving person will forgive, but Jesus says a forgiven person will know how to love. Sin itself, the anguish of alienation, the joy of reunion are all parts of the economy of salvation for Jesus:

"It is someone who is forgiven little who shows little love." Then he said to her, "Your sins are forgiven." Those who were with him at table began to say to themselves, "Who is this man, that he even forgives sins?" (Luke 7:47b–49)

Their worldview of meritocracy and cultic forgiveness has just been ignored. Somebody just lost their commission down at the Temple.

Jesus is transferring what was normally done in the Temple to the home. He is announcing the forgiveness of sins freely. This was normally tied up in a highly ritualized kind of religion at the Temple, "but he said to the woman, 'Your faith has saved you; go in peace'" (Luke 7:50). With that, Jesus redefines the boundaries—and availability—of holiness.

A Second Kind of Meal

The tradition of table fellowship shows up elsewhere in the Christian Scriptures—for example, the several loaves and fishes accounts in the Gospels (Matthew 14:13–21, 15:32–39; Mark 6:30–44, 8:1–10; Luke 9:10–17; John 6:1–13). Scholars say now that even while Jesus was still alive, there seemed to be two traditions of open table fellowship: one of bread and wine, the other of bread and fish. The bread and wine finally won out—that meal is what we call the Mass today in the Roman Catholic church.

But the bread and fish stories point to an open table fellowship tradition too. The exciting thing about these stories is that they emphasize surplus and outside guests. At the end of each of them, there are seven or twelve baskets left over. That surplus seems to be a point of this form of table fellowship. It's a type of meal we'd call a potluck supper today. Apparently, Jesus invited everybody to bring their food together and there was plenty for all the poor and then some.

It's unfortunate that we lost the bread and fish ritual meal, because the bread and wine ritual meal didn't emphasize this idea of surplus: real food that actually fed the poor. The bread and wine tradition lent itself more to cult and ritualization. The bread and fish tradition, if retained, might have contributed to issues of justice, community, and social reordering.

We see this after the resurrection, for example. In John 21:1–14, the apostles are out on the lake. They see Jesus on the shore, cooking fish at a charcoal fire. He invites them to come share bread and fish.

If we remember what happened after Jesus' arrest, we see the significance of this charcoal fire. The only other charcoal fire in the Gospels is where Peter stood when he betrayed Jesus (see John 18:18). Jesus invites him now to another charcoal fire, where they share the bread and the fish. And he says, in effect, "Peter, it's OK. Forget it." At this second charcoal fire, the risen Jesus initiates table fellowship with Peter, who just a few days before had rejected, betrayed, and abandoned him in his hour of need. It seems the bread and fish meal also had a healing, reconciling significance. What a shame we have lost this.

That passage opens the way for us to appreciate the familiar conflict in Paul's First Letter to the Corinthians. Written in the 50s CE, it shows how long the tradition of open table fellowship must have hung on.

> It is not the Lord's Supper that you eat; for when the eating
> begins, each one of you has his own supper first, and there is
> one going hungry while another is getting drunk. Surely you

have homes in which to do your eating and drinking? Or have you such disregard for God's assembly that you can put to shame those who have nothing? What am I to say to you? Congratulate you? On this I cannot congratulate you. (11:20–22)

Later eucharistic theologians don't know what to do with this text. Clearly, the first-century church had a very different understanding of Eucharist than we do now. Clearly, it was a sharing of real food, not a priest standing at an altar with bread and wine. We get that from the text. The explanation was that these were agape meals (ancient potlucks), not the real Eucharist. But very likely, the eucharistic celebration was joined to a meal. It was the potluck supper in which everyone came together. The rich people could bring rich food, the poor people would bring more humble offerings. Paul could be saying that it's not the Lord's Supper because the proper social arrangement is not there. If he's saying Jesus would not come to such a meal, this is revolutionary theology by later church criteria.

We really have no eyewitness accounts of the Last Supper. We have the Gospel accounts, but none of the twelve apostles who were at the Last Supper wrote the Gospels. The Gospels were written from the 70s to the 90s CE. Certainly, there was a good oral tradition. But it is very likely that the Last Supper was a Passover meal of open table fellowship—the final one of many among Jesus and his closest followers—that evolved into a ritualized offering of bread and wine. The disciples had come to understand it as a way of gathering, as the way to define their reality and their relationship to one another. It became for them a powerful symbol of unity, of giving and sharing, of breaking the self and giving over the self.

Yet the ritual became very succinct, as we see in our earliest record of the Eucharist:

For the tradition I received from the Lord and also handed on to you is that on the night he was betrayed, the Lord Jesus took some bread, and after he had given thanks, he broke it, and he said, "This is my body, which is for you; do this in remembrance of me." (1 Corinthians 11:23–24)

Then we get to the heart of Paul's argument for maintaining the new social order at Eucharist:

Everyone is to examine themselves and only then eat of the bread or drink from the cup; because a person who eats and drinks *without recognizing the body* is eating and drinking their own condemnation. (1 Corinthians 11:28–29, emphasis added)

Very possibly, the two traditions are coming together here: bread and wine plus potluck agape meal. Unfortunately, the second was lost, perhaps because of the very class difficulties it was trying to address. Yes, we are to recognize Jesus himself in the Eucharist, but we are also to recognize the living Body of Christ too. For the first thousand years, the Latin term *corpus verum*, the "true body," referred to the assembly. The people were the true Body of Christ in the assembly. When the true Body said through the mouth of the presider, "This is my body," the bread and the wine became the symbol of the living Body. The bread and wine were the *corpus mysticum*. These usages were completely reversed over time.

There is no Eucharist without an assembly. During the centuries of private Masses, we held onto that tradition (barely!) by requiring an altar boy. But clearly, the Eucharist was meant to be a sacrificial meal in which the Body recognized itself, defined itself, declared its social identity and its central purpose, which was to be Jesus in space and time, to live in a new world order of true sisterhood and brotherhood (meal), of redemptive suffering and solidarity (sacrifice).

Modern Implications

I want to close this chapter—and part one of this book—on a contemporary note. We need to consider and reconsider the symbolism of food in our own lives. In retreat houses and homes across the land, people are starting to reevaluate the social, political, economic, and nutritional meaning of food. America's love affair with beef, for example, and the disastrous effects that is having on the two-thirds world, have come under scrutiny in recent decades. Rain forests are being cut down, land and resources are being spent so that we can have burgers aplenty. (Now, of course, there are plenty of non-beef burgers to choose from!)

I was staying with a cattle rancher in California one time and, to his credit, he was reading a book describing the ill effects of cattle and beef production on the earth. The first day, he wasn't too happy with it. He came to speak with me the second night, troubled. He said to me, "Richard, I have to change my life." He saw that his livelihood could well be contributing to starvation overseas. That's reconnecting the two meals: Because of bread and wine, we must do "bread and fish" differently.

That's one contemporary way to consider this Gospel message. Food is still a way of being in solidarity with people. What we eat and what we don't eat can be a way of saying, "I want to be in solidarity with certain people who can't have meat three times a day." Meat is the food of the rich. It's the over-proteinization of people in a growing world of almost eight billion people.

Another example: Writer and poet Kathy Coffey compares the many acts of a woman, a loving mother and teacher, to the traditional words of institution at Eucharist. "In parenting," she writes, "'This is my body' becomes a constant refrain as time flows into launching healthy children: the buttoning, unbuttoning, listening, combing, bathing, encouraging, chauffeuring, story-reading and tucking-in processes of each day…. Into the children we parent, the students we teach…we pour ourselves."[22]

Of "This is my blood," she writes, in part: "When women gather to drink wine, the occasion is often festive. As the Chianti sparkles in the glasses, the laughter bubbles. Sometimes, then, we segue into the heartbreaks revealed only to the closest friends: the lost loves, the tragic betrayals, the spouses and children who disappoint, the talents wasted. From the shared sorrow emerges a new strength."[23]

After ten thousand meals, we begin to believe that we are *what* we eat, we are *who* we eat with, we are *where* we eat, we are *how* we eat, and, for believers, we are even *who* we eat: We have *recognized* the Body.

Understanding the Sermon

Where Jesus Is Heading

To clarify where Jesus is leading us, let me begin part two with what I hope is a demystifying explanation:

> **The old self on the old path:** Non-conversion or non-enlightenment.

> **The old self on a new path:** Where most religion begins and ends: new behavior, new language and practices that are sincere, but the underlying myth/worldview/motivation and goals are never really changed. My anger, fear, and ego are merely transferred to now defend *my* idea of God or religion.

> **The new self on a new path:** The total transformation of consciousness, worldview, motivation, rewards, and goals that characterizes *one who loves* and *is loved* by God. According to Jesus, this is conversion.

chapter six

Joining Heaven and Earth

L et's begin where the Gospels begin. In all four accounts, prominence is given to the character called John the Baptist. He is probably far more important than we have realized. John is Jesus' starting point too. That's what is symbolized by Jesus going to be baptized by John.

The beginning of Matthew 3 states that John the Baptist appeared and preached in the wilderness. This was his message: "Repent [which means "turn around"], for the Reign of Heaven is close at hand" (3:2). In Matthew's very next chapter, we will see that exact phrase become Jesus' first message: "Repent, for the Reign of Heaven is close at hand" (4:17b). Matthew's Jesus is obviously building on John, saying the same thing, but going further. It begins, much like religion, with duty or threat. In Jesus, it becomes invitation.

John "cries out" in the wilderness (see Matthew 3:3). That's wonderful symbolism, of course. Have you ever heard someone say to a child, maybe in a moment of desperation, "Talking to you is like talking to the wall! I might as well shout to the wind!" That's the telling symbolism of going out and yelling in the wilderness. No one in the establishment system wants to hear, or is willing to hear, what John has to say. He's radically questioning the very legitimacy of the existing religious order by doing religious practices on his own authority. John is the symbol of religion's need for constant reform, and the unhearable nature of the message.

The establishment sends people out to question John. He is a voice crying in the wilderness, apparently with some success. He refuses to wear the clothes of polite society, preferring clothing of camel hair with a leather belt around his waist. He does not eat the food of society. His food is locusts and wild honey. Notice there's something sweet and something bitter in John's scant, but symbolically rich, diet (see also Ezekiel 2:8–3:3). That is always the character of the wisdom figure: one who learns how to eat both. Wisdom puts together the yin and the yang, the day and the night. John has to eat both the sweetness and the tragedy of life.

Matthew's Gospel continues, "Then Jerusalem and all Judea and the whole Jordan district made their way to [John]" (Matthew 3:5). What we saw in part one explains why he would be a threat. These pilgrims are supposed to be making their way to Jerusalem and instead they're making their way out to hear this upstart in the desert! Among the crowd comes Jesus himself: "He came from Galilee...to be baptized by John" (3:13).

In effect, Jesus is legitimating what John is doing, saying it's OK to pour water over people and tell them their sins are forgiven. That's revolutionary. Jews were supposed to follow the Levitical Law of Holiness, and suddenly John is making it far too easy to get God to love them, to get God to forgive them. God becomes as available as Jordan River water. And, of course, the irony is that the water is in the desert, where water isn't supposed to be. In other words, we can find God everywhere—outside of institutions, official priesthood, or formal observance. I wonder if the church today even catches John's dangerous corrective.

Of course, Matthew the Evangelist had trouble with having Jesus baptized for the forgiveness of sin because in Matthew's understanding, Jesus had no sins to be forgiven. So, we have Jesus saying, "Leave it like this...it is fitting that we should, in this way, do all that uprightness demands" (3:15). Jesus doesn't have any trouble with this unofficial rite. He says, in effect, "I want to be a part of the whole human journey. I also agree with John's approach."

As soon as Jesus is baptized, there is a dramatic, mythologized statement of the eternal truth that is happening: He "came up from the water, and suddenly the heavens opened" (3:16b). What does it mean to have the heavens opening? It means two worlds become one, the sacred and the secular coming together: the joining of earth and heaven.

I've read the Book of Genesis from the time I was a child, but I marvel that there is always something new to learn. I was surprised to make a wonderful discovery one day: At the end of six days of creation it says, "And indeed it was very good" (1:31b). Only on one day does God *not* say the work was good: the second day, when heaven is separated from earth. This is the symbolic day when union was ripped apart, separating the sacred and secular, separating the holiness of God and the holiness of the earth.

The work of religion is to put together darkness and light, earth and heaven, and find they are one mystery. Christians' word for that is the Paschal Mystery, whereby we rejoin the separated worlds. Here we have Jesus, the great reconciler, coming to hold everything together. He walks the human path in all its demands, even submitting to this rite that John the Baptist has created.

That most basic and universal element, water, may be a natural religious symbol. I remember being in Varanasi (formerly Benares), the holy city of pilgrimage on the Ganges River in Uttar Pradesh State in northern India. In the early morning, there was dust as far as I could see. I remember the Hindus walking in hordes to the sacred river. There, they would strip naked and wash. Hindus believe that washing in the Ganges cleanses them of sin. Washing in water is a universal experience, and a powerful symbol for all renewal. Somehow, the spirit needs rituals to symbolize what's happening inside, to use the physical realm as well as ideas to fully experience metaphor. We cannot break through to the spiritual except through metaphor. We have to enact it, taste it, feel it.

Someone once said all great truths must be veiled; to look at truth directly blinds us. That's why religion has much more to do with poetry, song, and imagery than with academics. Take, for example, the Celts before we made Catholics out of them. The religion of Ireland was largely the memorization of poetry, nature religion, and fertility rites. In poetry, the metaphorical word has the power to break us through to comprehension of the symbol. The very word *symbol* means a "throwing together." In a Japanese haiku poem, for example, we see the eternal and we see the real, for just a moment, through the very precise and concise use of words.

Now we return to the symbol in Matthew: "And when Jesus had been baptized, he at once came up from the water, and suddenly the heavens opened and he saw the Spirit of God descending like a dove and coming down on him" (3:16). Note how the dove comes down from nowhere and alights on him. Grace cannot be created or manufactured from beneath; it always comes from beyond, from no certain place. Otherwise, it isn't grace. Try as we might, we cannot manufacture grace. It will always come from nowhere, for certain, like a dove coming out of the sky. It usually comes when we are in the midst of our sin or our busyness, so we know we didn't create it. *Grace* literally means "free."

Then comes Jesus' great conversion moment: "And suddenly there was a voice from heaven. 'This is my Son, the Beloved; my favor rests on him'" (Matthew 3:17). After this soul event, Jesus will move on his path. Nothing will stop him.

We know little about the time leading up to that moment. It will be a secret forever. What did Jesus do for thirty years? We don't know. Even the infancy accounts, which are only found in Matthew and Luke, don't really agree with one another. Mark and John didn't even find the infancy stories important enough to include in their Gospels. The point of the Gospels is that, at thirty, the man called Jesus came to know that he was a beloved Son. He came to know it all the way through, in his head, heart, gut; body, soul, and spirit. And, at that very point, curiously enough, Jesus is "led by the Spirit out into the desert to be put to the test by the devil" (4:1). A quick contrast, it seems.

It is crucial that Jesus is led by the Spirit. There are two wildernesses in the spiritual journey. We go into the first wilderness by our own stupidity, by our sin, blindness, ignorance, and mistakes. We all do that. But there's another wilderness, a darkness. The holy darkness is the darkness that God leads us into, through, and beyond. This darkness is necessary for the journey. In a certain sense, God's darkness is a much better teacher than light. There comes a time when we have to either go deeper into faith or we will turn back, when we have to live *without knowing* or lose faith altogether. So, we have the Spirit leading Jesus into the wilderness, to face the essential holy darkness.

Three Temptations

My understanding of the three temptations of Christ has shown up in my other writings. Yet some of it is worth touching on here because Matthew presents the temptations in the text (4:1–10) leading up to the Sermon on the Mount. The three temptations that Jesus must face are the necessary three temptations that every would-be believer, would-be evangelist, would-be Christian must face.

For me, they are summarized in this way: The first is the *desire to be effective or relevant*, to turn stones into bread (see 4:3), to see the fruits of our own action and to meet people's needs. Jesus has to give up that desire.

The second is the *desire to be right*: to "stand on the parapet of the Temple" (see 4:5). It's the desire to use God, to stand on religion for our own purposes. Jesus has to give up that assurance of being right—an ego need. It is very symbolic that it is the devil who has him stand on the Temple. It's also the only time in the entire Bible when the devil quotes Scripture. Matthew is showing us that we can use religion for diabolical purposes. Religion is both good and subject to misuse. Jesus' response is, in effect, "Don't play games with God" (see 4:7).

The third temptation is the *desire for power or control*, symbolized by the devil showing Jesus "all the kingdoms of the world and their splendor" (4:8b). Jesus is aware that power has many forms and many disguises in all of us. The devil names the common price for power: "Fall at my feet and do me homage" (4:9). Jesus rejects him with finality. "Then the devil left him" (4:11). Once we refuse to seek power in any form, there is not much that Satan can do to us.

These three demons are in all our lives: the desire to be effective, the desire to be right, and the desire to be powerful or in control. Until those demons have been faced and exorcised, we will very likely not preach the Gospel; we will preach our own selves.

It's only after Jesus exorcises these three demons that he sets out on his public ministry.

> As he was walking by the Lake of Galilee he saw two brothers, Simon, who was called Peter, and his brother Andrew; they were making a cast into the lake with their net, for they were fishermen. And he said to them, "Come after me and I will make you fishers of people." And at once they left their nets and followed him. (Matthew 4:18–20)

Did it happen exactly like that? The point is that Jesus gave people a major vision and challenge. He thus always appeals to risk-takers. Somehow, this man did fascinate people, and, with some ease, they left and followed him. But I find the next paragraph more confounding.

> Going on from there he saw another pair of brothers, James, son of Zebedee, and his brother John; they were in their boat with their father Zebedee, mending their nets, and he called them. (4:21)

Observe two things: First, they're with their father. There's the patriarchal family—James's and John's loyalties are clearly to Zebedee. Second, they are working. Those are the two sacred cows of kinship culture: family and occupation. You don't call those into question—yet Jesus does! "And at once, leaving the boat and their father, they followed him" (4:22).

Family and job are not bad things, but falling into easy patterns can keep us from asking new questions about life. (If we are open to love's demands, though, our family relationships can challenge us to the core.) It's significant that Jesus does not tell his followers to stop drinking and burn their *Playboys*—the hot sins—and *then* come and follow. He says, "Leave your father and your nets and come follow me *now*."

The Limits of Family

Jesus tells his followers to leave their families of origin because the families in which we grow up keep most people from asking bigger questions. Conventional family wisdom tells us to be nice kids in our hometowns and to do what nice kids in our hometowns do. For this reason, most religious founders tell people to leave their families. Call it a necessary detachment, a breaking away, to get a bigger worldview instead of just fulfilling Mama's and Daddy's dreams for us.

Does this mean we have to leave geographically? Not necessarily (although sometimes it can help). But, eventually, we must leave them spiritually, psychologically; we must look critically at their values and form our own—not necessarily opposed to theirs, but not accepting their values just *because* they are our parents'. It's a necessary part of growing up.

In male initiation rites worldwide, the boy is always taken away from his mother. Otherwise, he'll spend his whole life trying to please Mama or negatively reacting against her. The Catholic priesthood is filled with such men who became priests to please Mama (along with many other professions too, I'm sure). These men don't know who they are because that's not really their agenda. They're still living out of their mother's emotional world or doing something to please Dad so they'll finally get his approval.

I know a psychologist who thought she would be so happy when she got her PhD. She spent thousands of dollars and worked for years. A week after her graduation, though, she realized the only reason she did it was to get her dad to admire her. And her father didn't even come to the graduation. Now the degree means nothing to her.

Finding our soul is always about leaving our comfort zone: letting go and going to a bigger place. We can only ask the questions that our milieu allows us to ask. In many organizations, there are questions we cannot ask. Not that there's a law or formal policy, but if we really start asking certain questions, we might have to leave the company or the profession. Can business leaders be critical of maximizing profit at the expense of workers, communities, or the environment? Can a soldier question individual wars? Will people ever move beyond their families' emotional permissions? Can a woman choose simplicity or the single life if her parents want classy grandchildren?

Jesus creates the *ecclesia*: literally, "the called-out ones." The church should be that group of people who have moved to a place of freedom and are willing to ask the big questions of the extended family, not only the questions of the natural family.

Like it or not, Jesus in the Gospels says very little that's highly positive about the small family (see Matthew 10:37–39 or 12:46–50). Jesus broadens our vision. Ironically, the neoconservative movements today often hide behind the word *family*. Yet "family values" is sometimes a cover for a very self-protective and narrow agenda. This is true in Europe, in Latin America, and in the United States. For some reason, a positive buzzword is usually sufficient to cover up another agenda.

Jesus requires his first disciples to call into question even their families and family values. In our own time, we've discovered that call in a new way. Many people have recognized that if we don't break from a dysfunctional family, we become a part of the sickness ourselves. The Twelve Step movement has taught us to recognize what is sick about our families and what is good about them. For some, that means separating from the family, then freely entering back into it when there's the possibility of love and forgiveness. Leaving our "father" and our "nets" may also involve questioning our career choices, our family prejudices, and our class perspective.

Reclaiming Our Identity

"He went round the whole of Galilee teaching in their synagogues, proclaiming the good news of the Reign of God, and curing all kinds of disease and illness among the people" (Matthew 4:23).

Much of the Gospels is about either Jesus' preaching or his healing. With our modern, rational, scientific thinking, we may want to throw out all the healings and miracles of Jesus, but we can't. They are too central to the Gospels. My assumption is that power came out from Jesus. I believe that because I've seen so many physical healings in my own lifetime, and even in my own body (of a serious case of hypoglycemia at Lourdes in 1981 and of malignant melanoma after being prayed over and having surgery in 1992).

In the New Jerusalem Community, we had astounding healings that, to this day, I cannot explain. The most dramatic happened when the community was young. I was praying over a whole group of young people. A young woman with cerebral palsy, who had never before walked, easily stood up and walked straight toward me. To this day she walks, though with a limp. I *know* there is such a thing as physical healing. Yet, the Western scientific mind doesn't believe that anymore. We don't believe that when we pray over people, God's power sometimes comes through us and we are instruments for healing. Could it be that we don't believe in the active and contemporary power of Jesus in the world? (See James 5:14–15.)

There is always a latent social symbolism in Jesus' body miracles. That is not to say that the miracle didn't really happen. Jesus apparently performed hundreds of healing miracles. The ones chosen for the text always have layers of meaning. For example, a blindness miracle will follow an episode of the disciples' spiritual blindness. Jesus will be talking to his disciples, they won't get the point, and he'll heal someone who's deaf. There is the passage in Mark (5:26) where it says the woman with the hemorrhage had lost her whole life's savings to the medical profession. The healing story might well be a judgment on such injustice. In this case, *power goes out from him* (see Mark 5:30) like a laser beam finding its destination.

Jesus' miracles are acts of social protest, of taking back necessary power. He's telling the people, "You've got to own your own identity and purpose. Don't let the medical profession, the priestly or legal profession name you or own you." To this day, we surrender our God-given power to others, rather than understanding the gifts that have already been given us for spiritual health, physical health, and organizing our own lives. Jesus' innocuous word for this power is *faith*, and he usually praises people for it after they have moved beyond their victim stance.

The sick in Jesus' time were caught in a circle of double victimization. First, remember the tax system (see chapter four). They had to give at least two-thirds to the ruler and the ruling class and then live on the final third. There were other kinds of tolls and fees imposed even on the final third. People who are either poor or taxed into poverty are obviously not going to be able to afford good health care—even in Jesus' time. So bodily illness undoubtedly occurred in many people because they were oppressed and could not afford a doctor. Frankly, that is still the case for two-thirds of the world's population.

But then, to add insult to injury, the belief system at that time was that your sin made you sick (see John 9:2; Luke 13:1–5). As if that weren't enough, there were Temple fees, administered by the scribes, the religious lawyers, that were required to pay for the necessary ritual materials and animals in order to be made clean again. We could really call it *triple* victimization: forced poverty, false guilt, and then the financial hardship that came with the rituals that would return them to right relationship.

Let us return to the temptations for a moment. Notice that the first two temptations are preceded by this phrase: "If you are Son of God" (Matthew 4:3 and 4:6). It was perhaps Jesus' greatest temptation and his greatest act of faith: *If* you are Son of God….

That's the existential temptation that you and I face every day, the doubt as to *who we are*, where we came from, whether our names are written in heaven, whether we are children of God.

Jesus claimed and believed the divine image within him, and quite straightforwardly told us to do the same. That may be the whole Gospel in one sentence.

Repentance: "My Kingdom Go"

Jesus prefaces his announcement of the Reign of God with a strange word: *repent*. *Repent* is a throwaway word now. We see cartoons of prophets in sandwich boards that read, "Repent." It has this sort of corny, "churchy" meaning to it: "Beat yourself," or, "Get religion!"

The word is so misused, yet we don't dare throw it out. Just when many in the church have become ashamed of repentance, psychology and therapy have rediscovered it. If we don't repent—in other words, if we don't change—we die. If we don't repent of our past mistakes, we repeat them. We repeat them again and again and become very sick people. The addictive society understands this better than the church does now. Isn't that strange? The Twelve Step programs tell you to repent, to stop destructive behavior, but if I, as a priest, say "Repent," I'm accused of laying guilt on you. When we don't recognize what is wrong in our actions and understand why it is wrong, we are almost sure to do that wrong again, maybe just with a different pretext.

I've told gatherings in Germany that because there are Germans who have not completely repented the Second World War, they're destined to repeat it. It is as certain as the dawn that America will continue to be a militaristic, violent country because we have never repented any of our wars. In fact, we continue to turn to violence to address our divisions. Grief and repentance are the only appropriate Christian responses to *any* war—never a victory parade. At the very best, wars are a necessary evil, which we can never celebrate or romanticize. Perhaps we need "wailing walls."

I would like to state that the same ultimate reaction is perhaps true for divorce, abortion, and various forms of abuse: the appropriate healing and helpful response is probably some ritual of lamentation, sorrow, grieving, naming, forgiving, letting go, and going on. This useless shaming, blaming, and holding one another forever accountable for past mistakes all comes about, in my opinion, because secular culture has no way to repent. We are finding that the system, without a Gospel of healing repentance, is actually more unforgiving than the church ever was. All it has is the law, which kills, but Jesus has offered us the Spirit, which gives life (see 2 Corinthians 3:6).

Repentance is not an outdated concept. We must repent. *Metanoia* (*convertere* in Latin) means "to turn around." Jesus helped people to change, but he never tried to bully or shame them into it. I hope that we are going to learn from him in addressing many of our social and personal sins.

Reign of God Misperceptions

The concept of the Reign of God is absolutely central to Jesus. It is his core metaphor. If we don't understand the idea of the Reign of God, we don't understand Jesus' teaching, because much of Jesus' teaching is describing the Reign of God. Jesus repeats the words of John the Baptist, "Repent, for the kingdom of Heaven is close at hand" (Matthew 3:2, 4:17b).

The Greek word for kingdom in the Christian Scriptures is *basileia*. In our culture today, the word *kingdom* has sexist connotations for many. After all, kingdoms are run by kings, who can only be men. An equally valid translation for the word *basileia* (although it doesn't have many historical connotations because we haven't used it as much) is the "Reign of God." The important denotation is the issue of control, command, and oversight, having "a Lord" as organizing principle. Sometimes I sense that this is what a postmodern world actually resists and resents, even though the only real alternative is that I myself become the organizing principle.

In order to explain this concept of the Kingdom or the Reign of God, it may help first to say what it is not. The Reign of God—and this is the most frequent mistake—is not the same as heaven. The Reign of God is not where we go after we die: eternal life. Yet Christians of all denominations in the West use the term in this way. The scenario is something like this: You die; you go to Saint Peter, who has the keys to the gates of the Kingdom, and he lets you in. That idea is disproven by Jesus' very prayer: "Thy kingdom come, thy will be done *on earth* as it is in heaven." As always, Jesus is still joining earth and heaven.

"Thy kingdom come" means very clearly that the Reign of God is something that enters into this world, or, as Jesus puts it, "is close at hand." Don't project it into another world. It's a reality that breaks into this world now and then, when people are like God. The Reign of God is the Really Real. When the Really Real happens, when the true self emerges, we have a taste of what Jesus says it's all about. When that can happen in terms of structures or groups, when we have a free group of people who love the truth more than themselves, then we have a taste of the Reign of God descending to earth.

God gives us just enough tastes of the Reign of God to believe in it and to want it more than anything. It's always now-and-not-yet. If we review all the parables of Jesus discussed earlier, we'll see he never says the Reign of God is totally now or totally later. We only have the first fruits of the Reign of God in this world, but we get enough to know that it's the only thing that will ever satisfy us. For, once we have had the truth, we can't be satisfied with half-truths anymore. The Reign of God is the experience of the love of God, the ultimate and real truth. In its light, everything else is relative, even our own lives.

I hope you've met at least one Reign of God person in your life. They are surrendered people. We sense that life is OK at their core. They have given control to Another and are at peace. A Reign of God person lives for what matters, for life in its deepest sense. There's a kind of gentle absolutism about their lifestyle, a kind of calm freedom. Reign of God people seem like grounded, yet spacious, people. Whatever they are after, they already seem to be enjoying it—and seeing it in unlikely places. Reign of God people make us want to be like them. Mother Teresa (1910–1997) was an obvious and well-known example of this type of person; so was the Brazilian Archbishop Dom Hélder Câmara (1909–1999). Another was Anglican Archbishop Desmond Tutu (1931–2021) of South Africa.

But most Reign of God people lead much more ordinary lives. She might be a cashier at the grocery store who is joyful even under pressure. Her smile might be the inspiration that means hope for a single mother racing through the checkout line on her way to pick up kids at daycare and face an evening of childcare alone. He might be the real estate agent who, through his inner peace, conveys to a new family in town that everything will be all right. Reign of God people are anchored by their awareness of God's love deep within.

The second major mistake is the attempt to localize the Reign of God within one institution or one group or one place.

> Asked by the Pharisees when the Reign of God was to come, he gave them this answer, "The coming of the Reign of God does not admit of observation and there will be no one to say, 'Look, it is here! Look, it is there!' For look, the Reign of God is among you." (Luke 17:20–21)

The temptation of all churches is to believe they are the gathering of the saved, the born-again elite ones, on the right side of the eternal border. Yet

Jesus says the Reign of God is beyond clear observation. Like seasoning with salt or the action of leaven, it operates with invisible effect. No one possesses the Reign of God; it possesses us. We know we are merely a participant in a much larger mystery.

So, the Reign of God and church are not the same thing. The church is a means of pointing to the Reign of God, just as John the Baptist pointed toward the Lamb of God. When the church does not point beyond itself to eternity and God, but only tries to make us loyal to the church, it's entering into idolatry. Churches have done that in every age, and every church I know does it. That doesn't mean we leave the church; it means we need to have the humility to live in an imperfect world.

When we live in the Reign of God, we live in a liminal or "threshold space" between this world and the next. We learn how to live between heaven and earth, with one foot in each world, holding them preciously together. It will be a collision of opposites. If we try to hold those two worlds together, we will pay for it in our bodies. That's why Jesus says a Reign of God person must be prepared for persecution, because the world wants to ask for all our loyalty. Jesus always answers the Pilates of this world firmly, but without rancor: "My kingdom is not of this world" (see John 18:36). That is the necessary *not yet*.

In today's world, we are pressed to give our loyalty to the Stars and Stripes, to the Navy, to General Motors, or to whatever company employs us. The Reign of God person can't do that anymore. That's what we mean by the Lordship of Jesus Christ: If God is Lord, then the other systems of this world do not exercise first or final voice in our decisions.

Non-Idolatry

If I had to summarize the social teaching of Jesus in one phrase, it would be the doctrine of non-idolatry. Don't idolize anything. Even your marriage and your children are going to be taken from you. No form of government, no school of economics, no army or cause or country will ever be worth our whole soul. Serve God's world, but worship *nothing*. That is about as radical as we can get. Everything on earth is passing away. Spirituality is always about letting go. That's the rich, ultimate meaning of the word *forgiving*: handing it over before it is taken from us. We must fore-give all things.

There is no more radical teaching than the Reign of God. There are no more radical politics than the Reign of God. It makes relative every ideology, every loyalty, every addiction, every fascination, every attempt to affix our egos to this or to that. The Reign of God demands we recognize that all is passing away. It is the gate to perfect freedom. In the Reign of God, we're free for God, free for the truth—even in this world. Reign of God people are the salt of the earth, preservatives of *something more*. Like love, they make the world go round and keep the whole thing from self-destructing. Perhaps, like Abraham's ten just ones (see Genesis 18:32), they maintain the world in existence.

A Two-Level Teaching

We find a helpful and rather consistent pattern in the Synoptic Gospels: They usually address the same crowds on two levels at the same time. Whether we stand at the bottom or perceive ourselves to be at the top, the Scriptures both challenge and console us all. This makes for a good Scripture study, and I recommend that you check it out for yourself.

In each situation, there seems to be a Gospel for the oppressors and some good news for the oppressed too. I suspect that we are all in both positions at different times and in different groupings, but we each need liberation and truth. To those who have the power, the control, the answers, Jesus is always saying, "Come down!" as he did to Zacchaeus, a wealthy senior tax collector. "Zacchaeus, come down. Hurry, because I am to stay at your house today" (Luke 19:5). The issue quickly becomes one of justice and restitution. Many times, however, the elders, high priests, and scribes refuse to "come down" from their judgments and their prepackaged conclusions. You can't fault Jesus for trying, however.

In the Gospels, the greatest number of people seem, instead, to be on the bottom: the sick, the outcasts, the indigent, the public sinners, the foreigners in a Jewish culture, the women in a patriarchal culture. To these, Jesus' message is unrelenting and consistent: "Come up!" There are a number of one-liners from Jesus that did not win him many friends among the comfortable: "Your faith has restored you to health; go in peace" (Mark 5:34b); "In no one in Israel have I found faith as great as this" (Matthew 8:10b); or "those now last...will be first, and those now first...will be last" (Luke 13:30). On both sides, the reaction of "nice people" is outrage, scandal, and sometimes even a plot to kill him.

I would interpret Jesus' strategy in this way: If you have been at the bottom, he assumes that you might have learned the lessons of powerlessness and humility (done the First Step, as the Twelve Step crowd would say), and he is quite anxious for you to experience instead your dignity, goodness, and inner power. He is always quite lavish and immediate with his affirmations—even without checking someone's denominational affiliations or marital status. (Seems like there might just be a lesson hiding in there somewhere!)

But Jesus never courts the favor or patronage of those who are riding their high horse. His challenges are immediate and, by our humanistic standards, even harsh. I doubt whether we could, or even should, try the same method because we would then be jumping into the same saddle of superiority, but we must retrieve the prophetic level of the Gospel. Ever since Constantine, the church has been coddling the powers that be, hoping to win their favor for the new Catholic high school fund drive. Unfortunately, the Gospel agenda does not influence the new high school nearly as much as the new high school determines what Gospel we are even willing to consider. We have been in this dilemma for some centuries now, clergy and laity alike. Religious life was supposed to provide a way out, but now the religious are often assimilated too.

I always wondered why we had feast days and institutions named in honor of Christ the King, many statues and crosses of Christ the Priest, but I have never in all the Catholic world met a celebration or picture in honor of Christ the Prophet. Something is out of balance.

chapter seven

The Path of Transformation

No matter what religion or belief system people may hold, underneath it all there are three possible worldviews: The universe is against us, the universe is for us, or the universe is neutral.

The latter states that reality is indifferent: It is neither for us nor against us. There is no God against us or for us; we're basically on our own in the universe. There are plenty of people in plenty of churches who subscribe to this worldview: "There probably is a God, and God might even be just and good, but this God is not actively involved in our lives or history." That worldview makes for very dead churches.

People can formally be Christian, Hindu, Buddhist, or anything else and go through all the rites and services. But, if the grace of God hasn't moved into the conscious and unconscious levels and really touched them—which is the full meaning of conversion—they can keep the formulas in their heads but have no real awareness of the divine.

That's the malaise of Western Christianity today. People keep up the external observance of reliance upon God, while underneath they depend only on themselves. "Nothing's going to happen unless I make it happen," they say to themselves. There is no active trust in the presence or the reality of God, or that God makes any real difference.

This form of secularism is malicious, because we can't get at it. All the right words and ideas are there—the person goes to church, is born again or gets confirmed—but beneath it all there is the sense of an indifferent universe and an indifferent, distant God.

Over the years, I have been partially critical of the charismatic movement, but I want to state something very positive about it too. Their "baptism in the Holy Spirit" was an experience of God being actively involved in the world. I'm amazed how many people I meet today, in various social ministries throughout the country, who will reveal, sometimes after a beer at night, that they were in a prayer group some years ago. They say it almost as if they're ashamed. Yet, for many people, that experience helped them get the Gospel out of their heads and into their guts. It seems that unless Pentecost happens, most people remain in an indifferent universe. They have no active sense of God being a co-creator who is really involved in their daily lives.

If people stay in the indifferent universe for long, they usually move to the second worldview, where people perceive reality as hostile, destructive, or judgmental. Not only is God not involved but, in fact, God has to be appeased. There are plenty of actively religious people who are appeasing God. For those people, God is somehow against us: watching us, judging us, critiquing us, certainly not on our side, but making sure we jump the hoops, making sure that we somehow must win God's favor. Many Christians, even clergy and religious with whom I've worked over the years, don't want to believe that way, but it's clear that they do by the fearful way they live.

They don't see God as being on their side, but almost as an opponent or nagging critic. It's probably highly symbolic that Pentecost comes fifty days after the sacramental experiences of Holy Thursday. People can be churched, or even ordained, and not believe that God is fire within them.

Most people's operative God image, in the early stages, is a combination of their mom and their dad, although most are unaware of it. Many of those who trust early and deeply in God had strong, nurturing parents. But if their dads were hostile, if their mothers were inconsistent, or they felt they could not trust either parent—basically, that all gets transferred to God. Either way, child-parent relationships become foundations for our relationship with God.

Until we have moved to a level of prayer and surrender, where God and grace are allowed to invade the subconscious—not just conscious—belief systems, it really doesn't matter, in some ways, what our conscious belief systems are. Until we get God into the subconscious, where our deep agendas are touched and freed, our formal religion doesn't make a lot of difference. We can still have an indifferent, or even a hostile, destructive, or judgmental worldview. It will show itself in fear, strong control needs, or the "going through the motions" that characterize an awful lot of churchgoers.

The third worldview can only be given by grace. It's given a great head start by loving, non-invasive parents who themselves believe in a benevolent universe. For this group, the universe is not against us, nor is it sitting out there, indifferent to human needs. Somehow, it's even on our side. Reality can be trusted. We don't need to pull all the right strings or push all the right buttons; grace is everywhere. It's good to be here. Life is perhaps difficult, but it is still good and trustworthy at the core.

Carl Jung wrote of synchronicity, Christianity speaks of providence, Hinduism references karma. Somehow, they're all suggesting a benevolent universe in which the foundation of all things is love. No matter how tragic things get, love can be trusted; we're standing in a solid universe. God is in charge and this God is good and involved. Pentecost has happened, just as with Jesus in the desert.

Until we meet a benevolent God and a benevolent universe, until we realize that the foundation of all is love, we will not be at home in this world. That meeting of God, that mystical experience, cannot be communicated by words. We either have it or we don't. It is a gift of participation in the very life of God. Its inherent character is best described by three overlapping characteristics: faith, hope, and love. We rightly call them the supernatural virtues because they are a "participation in the very life of God"[24] as opposed to a natural talent.

In the early chapters of Matthew, Mark, and Luke, Jesus undergoes a conversion. He is baptized, then goes to the desert. We don't know what happened to Jesus in the desert, but he comes out obviously believing in a loving universe that can be trusted. His insight is summarized in that wonderful phrase, "You are my beloved Son." The experience of being a beloved child is the experience of living in a loving universe: I am beloved, I am taken care of, I am believed in.

Anxiety is what reveals our real belief system. If we are anxious—if we are worried about many things, to use Jesus' phrase (Matthew 6:25–34 counsels against worry five times!)—then we're still in one of the first two universes. If God isn't on our side, we've got to fix and control our world. Why wouldn't we? Who else is going to? Many people's religion is an obsession with security—and not just economic security: security of reputation, status, image. If we are still securing ourselves or using religion to maintain or justify the self, our operative image of God is still an indifferent or hostile God. Don't be anxious about that either! We all start there, and the love-trust relationship grows over time.

Jesus' Definition of Faith

As a priest, I will meet people in airplanes who invariably throw out this phrase: "Oh, don't get me wrong, Father. I believe in God." As a priest, that's not my concern. That's not what Jesus is concerned about. Belief in God has been the primordial tradition since the beginning of time. Ninety-nine point nine percent of people who have ever lived on this earth have believed in God. Atheism is a modern, rational phenomenon of the Western world—a little blip on the screen. Of course there's a God! That's not even worth wasting time on. Faith, for Jesus, is *not* the opposite of not believing in God.

After assuring me that they believe in God, people on airplanes will add, "Well, I try to be good. Now, I don't go to church very much." Frankly, I don't think Jesus would really care. Going to church is not the issue either.

For Jesus, faith is not opposed to not believing in God. It doesn't mean you go to church, or that you're into religion, or that you say, "Lord, Lord!" (see Matthew 7:21). Faith for Jesus is *the opposite of anxiety.* If we are anxious, if we are trying to control everything, if we are worried about many things, we don't have faith, according to Jesus. We do not trust that God is good and on our side. We are trying to do it all ourselves, lift ourselves up by our own bootstraps.

The giveaway is *control.* That's a good litmus test of the quality of our faith. People of faith don't have to control everything, nor do they have to change people. We have the wisdom to know the difference, as the Twelve Step people say. We cannot "fix" the soul. "Set your hearts on the Reign of God first, and on God's saving justice, and all these other things will be given you as well. So do not worry about tomorrow; tomorrow will take care of itself" (Matthew 6:33–34a).

I usually say that if people are humble and honest, I really know they will be all right. If either humility or honesty is missing, they've got some spiritual work to do. Of course, we can grow in humility and grow in honesty, but if the seed is there, grace is going to keep invading and breaking through. God is for us more than we are for ourselves. All we can do is be open. The One who created us cares like a parent for a child (see Isaiah 49:15). God cares for creation in an irrational way, a way that has nothing to do with logic, worthiness, or correct behavior. We are cared for simply because we are beloved children. Paul expresses the same truth with the concepts of birthright and inheritance (Romans 8:14–17; Galatians 4:5–7; Ephesians 1:14). John simply describes it as the divine choice for our friendship, not our servitude (John 15:15–16).

Three Themes of Jesus

Three consistent themes recur in Jesus' teaching. (I'm relying here on the scholarship of Marcus Borg [1942–2015] in his wonderful book *Jesus: A New Vision*.) The first is *a new image of reality that challenges conventional wisdom*. I hope the whole of this book is an assault on that conventional wisdom. Jesus seems to think it is this very "normalcy" that keeps people from the banquet, more than the so-called "hot sins."

Conventional wisdom crucified Jesus. Then, as now, it was conventional wisdom that kept people from God. We think of wicked vices as keeping people from God, and indulging a vice certainly does. But people who are "into" the hot sins are often the ones who really hunger and thirst for justice. In the Gospels, these are the people who really seem to come around and get the truth.

But the conventional-wisdom people, who are trying to control it all and trying to be nice and proper, don't realize that they need to hunger and thirst for anything. I believe that's the meaning of the "sin against the Holy Spirit" that Jesus says cannot be forgiven (see Matthew 12:32). The reason it cannot be forgiven is that it would never enter our minds that we have anything that needs to be forgiven! There's no asking for forgiveness, no recognition of being trapped. Conventional wisdom—status-quo culture that refuses to "turn around"—assures the group that they're elite, correct, the norm, that they do it well and swell.

Jesus talks about the broad way and the narrow way in Matthew 7:13–14. The broad way is conventional wisdom, I believe—the groupthink, cultural mood, collective sleepwalking—that many take and that leads to destruction. Jesus describes the narrow gate, conversely, as a rough road that few discover, but that "leads to life"—obviously not conventional wisdom.

Jesus' second theme, to use a medical term, is *a diagnosis of the human condition*. Jesus is describing what it means to be a human being, what all people are up against. Notice, to say *diagnosis* is not to say an *answer* (although Jesus finally *lives* an answer). Human life is a path, and the path will be partially death and partially joyous life. Trust the path. Let it unfold and see God in it. The human condition has an essentially tragic character that logic, riches, or even science will never be able to erase. The same is true for happiness, which Jesus defines in a totally extraordinary way in Matthew 5:1–12 (as we will see in the next chapter). Jesus is content, it seems, to *describe* the human dilemma with insight, patience, and compassion. Somehow, that feels like an answer. It is.

The third consistent theme of Jesus is a description of *how transformation happens*, both for the person and for society. We have not been very good students of Jesus concerning personal transformation, emphasizing instead a kind of stoic "grin and bear it." As we would therefore expect, our teaching on the transformation of institutions, structures, and society has been even worse. Not ready for his doctrine of non-idolatry, we have sequentially put all our hope in the Roman Empire's favor, feudal lords, the divine right of kings, European culture, anti-Communism, capitalism, and democracy. I think the last one is about to disappoint us too.

Transformation, though, is not the same as change. Change is when something new begins. Transformation is just the opposite: It happens, more often than not, when something old falls away. It happens after a crisis, when something we've learned to depend upon is taken away. Not all crises, of course, lead to transformation. When something is taken away that we've grown used to or addicted to, we will either turn bitter or be transformed.

Anyone reading this book has lived in a period of human history that has seen more change than any other century ever. We've undergone psychological change, cultural change, political change, economic change, and worldview change. Most people throughout history (except during times of plagues or violent upheavals) have lived their lives inside one paradigm or model. Most people agreed upon one worldview. Yet there have been major paradigm shifts four or five times over the past century! Maybe that's why we have so many unhealthy people now. There has been massive change, but the change has not always been accompanied by transformation.

When change is demanded, yet is unaccompanied by the transformation of the soul, people are often destroyed. To be honest, most people don't age very well. Transformation is required to understand the changes that life asks of us, to resituate ourselves in the world. The function of all mythologies, stories, and religion is to hold together our lives in a meaningful universe. Every culture has both its creation stories and a story of the end, toward which all is tending. As Christians, we have the creation story of Genesis and the second coming of Christ as the Omega point.

These stories, usually picked up by osmosis in a healthy family and in healthy religion, situate us inside of a safe and meaningful universe. Just as the body needs food, so the soul needs meaning, and the spirit needs ultimate meaning. Some have called this "the Cosmic Egg," inside of which people can find rest and even happiness. Unless we know where it all came from and where it is all going, we tend to be anxious, incoherent, and as changeable as the weathervane. This is the burden of modern secularism, and I'm sure the source of much mental and emotional illness in our society. As Jean Houston has noted, "When mythic material remains latent, unused and unexplored, it can lead to pathological behavior."[25] For much of the postmodern world, the Cosmic Egg has not just cracked; it is gone altogether. In fact, many would deny any universal meanings or patterns. *The* Story does not exist. All we can do is create our own moments of significance and meaning. It is all pretty fragile, as is the modern self.

The Cosmic Egg

THE STORY

OTHER STORIES

OUR STORY

MY STORY

Because this is so lonely and probably impossible to live with, many at least move to a second level of "our" story. At least we can find value and meaning in our communal identities—our nationality, our ethnicity, our religion, our club or motorcycle gang. This takes away some of our private anxiety, but it is interesting how even group identities have moved in the direction of pathology. Support groups now fill our church basements for everything from gamblers anonymous and survivors of breast cancer to parents of children who eat too much. Some say that such groups gather more people than the church proper. At any rate, Our Story is surely worthwhile, and we are grateful that people are discovering some language of community and interdependence. On the downside, it is also at the level of gangs, militias, ethnic violence throughout the world, and a lot of psychobabble that is going nowhere.

In general, we could say that many sophisticated, educated, and progressive types tend to get trapped in the language of My Story, whereas many conservative and group-think folks tend to get trapped in Our Story. The first become individualists because that is their first and final language: what *I* feel or think. The second become ideologues: loving explanations more than concrete people. Both are a clear avoidance of The Story, what Jesus would call the Reign of God, the world of right relationships.

Again, the inclusive and holistic nature of the Reign of God is that it not only includes My Story and Our Story, but actually demands that we take them both seriously—because God does. Thus the private journey and the collective history of Israel make up the Bible. For us, theology and anthropology are the same thing. The Story builds upon *my* personal experience and *our* historical experience as a people, and gives us the only language by which we can understand the great and eternal patterns.

The Bible is not a listing of clear spiritual conclusions, although we would surely like that now and then. The Bible, instead, is a "text in travail"[26] which invites us into the tension and journey itself. The Bible is a recorded history of what happens to human beings when they meet the True Sacred, the ways they avoid and deny Transcendence, and all the ways that they flirt with false transcendence. "Jump in," it says, and then you will know the Bible is inspired because the patterns are yours too. You will not believe most of it by faith, but by experience. Hear the phrase in a new way now: "The Bible is *always* true."

The Bible reveals patterns of truth, however, that are from beyond the pale. They are not the patterns that cultures of money, power, or religion will naturally perceive. It seems they have to break in or "be revealed" from outside the system. These pattern stories become very explicit in the teachings of Jesus, although in most cases he is building upon his Jewish roots. He tries to make visible and explicit the patterns that are already there, but that we can't see. No wonder that he seems like a total traditionalist and a wild reformer at the same time. We find this creative tension is itself the *path of transformation*. A Spirit-led person always knows how to put the two together, whereas tiny minds and hearts fall into cracks on either side of the path. I will share four of the big patterns, the "great themes" as I called them in my early audiocassettes in the 1970s. These stories make up The Story that is always true (but doesn't look true before we have walked it).

The Great Themes

Exodus and Easter: Life and death is the unavoidable pattern of growth and transformation. It is redemptive when trusted as God's way. It is the only sign Jesus says he will give: the sign of Jonah, the Paschal Mystery, the folly of the cross, exile and return.

A bias toward the bottom: Starting with enslaved Semites, then choosing the barren, the old, the last son, the rejected, the alien, the outcast, the sinner, the victim Jesus, the Bible reverses all human expectation.

No correlation between gifts and worthiness: With great and continuing difficulty, the Bible moves the focus from attainment to acceptance, from hard work to soft surrender, from "I am worthy" to "God is good." All is gratuitous. This fights all self-centered logic.

Letting go:

"I will deliver you. You have only to keep still" (Exodus 14:14). This becomes the faith theme throughout the Bible (*letting go of control*).

"Do not be afraid" is the most frequent line in the Bible (*letting go of fear*).

Yahweh your God will be your strength. "Cut off from me, you can do nothing" (John 15:5) (*letting go of the small self*).

Most of Jesus' teaching is about one thing: forgiveness, which is the great and necessary thawing of all human history (*letting go of hurts*).

Thus we are taught that the path of transformation is very different than we might have imagined. The Bible gives us not a language of ascent, not a search for spiritual superiority, not a disciplined attainment of higher states of consciousness (Gnosticism is a heresy that has been condemned in new forms in every century!), but exactly the opposite. The Bible gives us a language of descent, a search for who we already are, a releasing into an ordinary—and already extraordinary—humanity.

Our ordinary lives are given an extraordinary significance when we accept that our lives are about something much larger, our pain is a participation in the redemptive suffering of God, our creativity is the very passion of God for the world. No longer do we need to self-validate, self-congratulate, or self-doubt—our place in the cosmos is ensured. I do not need to be in the whole play or even understand the full script. It is enough to know that I have been chosen to be one actor on the stage. I need only play my part as well as I can.

Did you know that the word *disaster* comes from the Latin word meaning "to be disconnected from the stars"? The stars represented the great story, the universal story. Our lives are usually a disaster unless we live under these stars. We live our little story under the great story. As long as we know that our little story—that little life of getting married and having children and dying in Omaha, Nebraska—as long as we know it's tied up to the big story, we will be sane and basically happy. Psychology and therapy cannot give us such a cosmology; only religion can.

What we have today in the West, as probably in no other time in human history, is the disconnection between our little stories and a great universal story. We don't believe the big story. We're lost in insignificance. Those of us who were raised in the old Roman Catholic Church know it wasn't always that way. However we might criticize the Church before 1960, however we might think poorly of it now, it did something marvelous for most people. If you were raised well as a little Catholic girl or boy, you were told stories that tied you to a cosmic, coherent, and compassionate universe.

I still remember sitting in the first grade, listening to Sister Charlotte Marie, a wonderful woman, tell us the story of Bethlehem. It's the story we hear every Christmas and see on countless Christmas cards. Think of how children listen to stories: with their mouths open in awe. To them, it's all real. Then, as Christmas came, my parents would take me up to see the crib in the church and I could see it happening, just as in the story. A child has no doubt that this is what Mary and Joseph, Baby Jesus and the shepherds looked like. It's high drama and wonderful.

As Epiphany approached, the three kings started marching across the sanctuary. We couldn't wait to get into the church on January 6. The shepherds would be gone and the three kings would be standing there. And we thought that's exactly the way it was two thousand years ago. God came into the world. God was a little baby who's just like us, with Mary, a loving mother, and Joseph, a loving father. The whole universe was rejoicing in his birth.

That's a benevolent universe. It's safe to live in this world. Jesus is poor, but the world is still his chosen home. It is all right to be poor, to be human, and to be *here*. "I think I'll live!" we might conclude. That's how religion, first of all, *saves us*.

Jesus starts his Sermon on the Mount by talking about happiness (see Matthew 5:3–12). The people I know who are happy always have a simple belief system. It's very concrete, it's personal, and they don't refashion it every week according to the latest polls or the cultural mood. The happiest people alive usually believe one or two things very strongly and base their whole life on that. Let's look at these few happy secrets.

chapter eight

The "Happy Attitudes": Salt and Light

Matthew sets the stage for the Sermon with three simple sentences: "Seeing the crowds, he went onto the mountain. And when he was seated, his disciples came to him. Then he began to speak" (5:1–2a). Remember, Moses came down from the mountaintop. Matthew's message is clear: This is the new Moses going back to the mountaintop, reproclaiming the truth, bringing down the new law. That is a very important context. In a certain sense, the Sermon is the replacement of the Ten Commandments.

The "happy attitudes" ("congratulations" would be our secular equivalent) or Beatitudes, as we traditionally call them, are addressed not to the crowds, but to Jesus' disciples. That's a clue to how important the happy attitudes are. It's only the smaller group of disciples who are prepared to hear this challenging sermon. The heaviest stuff in the Gospel—"taking up the cross"—is addressed not to the crowds or the disciples, but to the inmost circle of the twelve apostles. The Sermon is addressed to the second circle of disciples, who are still being initiated. That's us!

There is a very real plan in Jesus' initiation, it seems. He is aware of timing, readiness, and maturation. At the early stages, we are not ready for the hard Gospel; we can't hear about the cross. I would say that most people under the age of thirty have a hard time understanding the cross because the ego is saying, "Grow, grow, grow; become, become, become." We can't walk into a twenty-one-year-old's life and say, "Die." Dying doesn't make sense to a young person. But something happens to us as we grow older. Some are in their thirties or forties when the truth starts sinking in: Dying is a part of life. By fifty or sixty, we must learn that dying is not opposed to life; it's a part of a greater mystery—and we are a part of that mystery. The older psyche is ready to hear such sober truth.

"How blessed are the poor in spirit: The Reign of Heaven is theirs." (Matthew 5:3)

What an opening line! I always say it's the opener for the inaugural address. "How happy are the poor in spirit." It's crucial, a key to everything Jesus is teaching, or it wouldn't be the opener. It is hard to imagine that a saying so radical should become so familiar, so normal. It does appear that Matthew has chosen to soften it from the more original phrase that we see in Luke and the noncanonical Gospel of Thomas. We find the more primitive Beatitudes in Luke 6:20–49. Luke's Gospel is for the poor, so he leaves the hard words of Jesus as scholars believe they were originally spoken: "How blessed are you who are poor" (6:20a). The counterpoint is also listed: "But alas for you who are rich" (Luke 6:24a). There's no softening of things in Luke.

That's not to fault Matthew, who's a smart man. He's addressing a nice, middle-class community, folks who have good jobs in the business community or the defense labs, as it were. He'd better not just say "poor" or they'll walk out on the talk. So, he says, "Happy are the poor *in spirit.*" The truth is still there: Poor in spirit means to live without a need for our own righteousness. It's inner emptiness; no outer need for our own reputation. If we are poor in spirit, it won't be long before we are poor. In other words, we won't waste the rest of our life trying to get rich because we know better.

There are a number of scriptural words that describe the different states of poverty. Christian Scripture scholars point out that the normal Greek word used for the peasant class is *tapeinoi*, but that is not the word Matthew and Luke use here. They use the word *ptochoi*, which would apply not to the 80 percent in the peasant class but to the eighth and ninth classes: the unclean and those who are expendable (see chapter four). *Ptochoi* literally means "the very empty ones, those who are crouching." They are the bent-over beggars, the little nobodies of this world who have nothing left. Jesus is saying, "Happy are you, you're the freest of all." James, traditionally believed to be the brother of Jesus, uses the same word in his letter: "It was those who were poor according to the world that God chose to be rich in faith and to be the heirs to the Reign of God which he promised to those who love him" (James 2:5b). Maybe they were taught such wisdom by their own family and lifestyle.

The higher up we are in the system, the more trapped we are. The more we are outside the system, the freer we are. Everyone knows that for every promotion or recognition we accept, there is a price: more party line! That is surely true for business and almost any organization, including the church. There's a cynical joke among priests: "A bishop never gets two things: a bad meal or the truth."

The point is that when we are high up in anything, we are expected to represent it, hold it together, and affirm it. Why not? We would likely be irresponsible if we didn't. So, the spiritual greats, like Jesus, just say, "Avoid it!" When we go to a party, most of us want to be slapped on the back by the gang, to be a part of the old boy network (and yes, there is an old girl network too). It's not that people who want to be accepted are bad. It's just that we want Bob to like us, so we tend to say what Bob wants us to say. The price of the truth can be very great: We say what is needed to survive and to be liked inside the group, and to hold the group in unity.

"How blessed are the poor in spirit" (Matthew 5:3a), the little ones who don't have to play any of these games. Jesus is recommending a social reordering here, quite different from common practice. Notice how he also uses present tense: "The Reign of heaven *is* theirs" (Matthew 5:3b, emphasis added). He doesn't say *"will be* theirs." That tells us, once again, that the Reign of God isn't later. It's present tense: We *are* the free ones now, if we remain without anything to protect or anything we need to prove or defend.

I know people who have left Christianity to become Buddhists precisely because of the doctrines of emptiness, simplicity, and nonviolence that they discovered in Buddhist teaching. If only they had been taught these same foundations in Jesus' Beatitudes!

"Blessed are those who mourn: They shall be comforted." (Matthew 5:4)
On men's retreats, we speak of grief work. There is a therapeutic, healing meaning to tears. Undoubtedly that's true, even as we study what's in tears. We speak of salt in tears, but now there's evidence of washed-out toxins. Is not weeping, in fact, necessary? Beyond that, of course, Jesus is describing the state of those who weep, who have something to mourn about. They feel the pain of the world. Jesus is saying that those who can grieve, those who can cry are those who will understand.

The Syrian Fathers Ephraim (d. 373) and Simeon (390–459) weren't as popular as the Greek Fathers in the early centuries of the church. The Greek Fathers tended to filter the Gospel through the head; the Syrians' theology—like a lot of modern-day feminist theology—is much more localized in the body. The Syrian Fathers, in effect, wanted tears to be a sacrament in the church. Saint Ephraim went so far as to say that until we have cried, we don't know God. How different!

We think we know God through ideas. Yet corporeal theology, body theology, indicates that weeping perhaps will allow us to know God much better than through ideas. In this Beatitude, Jesus praises the weeping class, those who can enter into solidarity with the pain of the world and not try to extract themselves from it. That is why Jesus says the rich man can't see the Reign of God. The rich one spends life trying to make tears unnecessary and, ultimately, impossible.

Weeping over our sin and the sin of the world is an entirely different mode than self-hatred or hatred of others. The weeping mode, if I can call it that, allows us to carry the dark side, to bear the pain of the world without looking for perpetrators or victims. Instead, we recognize the tragic reality in which both sides are trapped. Tears from God are always *for everybody*, for our universal exile from home. "It is Rachel weeping for her children, refusing to be comforted" (Jeremiah 31:15b).

That might seem ridiculous, and it is especially a stumbling block for men in our culture. To men's groups, I say that the young man who cannot cry is a savage; the old man who cannot laugh is a fool. But something in our culture has told young men not to cry because that will make us look vulnerable. So, we men stuff our tears. We die, by the way, on average, many years earlier than women. Could there be a connection? It seems likely. We must teach all young people how to cry. In the second half of my life, I understand why Saints Francis and Clare cried so much, and why the saints spoke of "the gift of tears."

"Blessed are the gentle: They shall have the earth as their inheritance." (Matthew 5:5)

This Beatitude is a quote from Psalm 37:11: "The humble shall have the land for their own." Some translate "gentle" as "the nonviolent." The translation perhaps most familiar is "the meek." There's irony here. If there was one hated group in the Palestine of Jesus' day, it was landlords—those who possess the land. Nobody possessed land except by violence, by oppression, by holding onto it and making all the powerless peasants pay a portion of their harvest. Jesus is turning that around and saying, "No, it's you little ones who are finally going to possess the land." It's said with sarcasm, with irony, but with hope.

Jesus is undoubtedly redefining the meaning of land, building on what every Jew would have known. Hebrew Scripture teaches that only God possesses the land (see Psalm 24:1; Leviticus 25:23). In the jubilee year, all the land was to be given back to its original occupants (see Leviticus 25:8–17). The Native Americans understood the freedom of the land, yet Western society cannot. Private property forces us behind fences, boundaries, and walls. We actually think that we "own" the land because there's a deed down at the courthouse. Isn't that strange? It's all cultural. People closer to the earth know that only God possesses the earth, that we're all stewards, pilgrims, and strangers on the earth.

Possession is an illusion in the light of the Reign of God. What do you possess? Wait a few years—we'll see how much you possess when you're six feet under! We don't *possess* anything. But that sounds ridiculous unless we understand The Story. Once we understand The Story, we know that possession is a passing illusion. The meek know that landlords, flood, or drought can quickly take the land back.

This image of meekness is the one Saint Francis embraced. He told us Franciscans never to own anything so that we can be open to everything. There is a strain of this thinking in the American tradition of free public libraries and art museums. We don't have to buy art and bring it home to our house to possess it. It's everywhere, all around us. Personal ownership is not necessary for enjoyment. Why can't it be everybody's sculpture or painting? Why can't it be in a common place where we all can look at it?

In most areas of our lives, though, we think that we have to bring things into our homes to possess them. After a while, our things possess us.

"Blessed are those who hunger and thirst for justice: They shall have their fill." (Matthew 5:6)

Most Bibles to this day will soften this Beatitude: "hunger and thirst for what is right" or "for righteousness" are the more common translations. That's a softer, more religious message. The word in Greek clearly means "justice." Notice that the concept of justice is exactly halfway through the Beatitudes and appears again at the very end. It's a couplet, stating, "This is the point: To live a just life in this world is to have identified with the longings and hungers of the poor, the meek, and those who weep." This identification and solidarity are already a profound form of social justice. This Beatitude is surely both spiritual *and* social.

Much as Matthew tries to soften it for his middle-class audience, he really can't soften Jesus' central message. It's still unsettling and most extraordinary. "Make sure you're not satisfied" is the message. "Keep yourself in a state of deliberate dissatisfaction." Contemplatives know this. In contemplation, we can't always say we have met God, or that we have come to some great insight after praying. What real prayer does is stir holy desire, but not always satisfy it. As the unconscious bubbles up, we find out what it is we really desire. First, we move through the layers of superficial desire. Both addiction counselors and spiritual directors will tell us that when we respond to a need with a substitute, it only intensifies the need.

At first, it might be a new house, a new set of clothes, a new image that we think we desire. We might think that by getting a new set of clothes, we are going to be happy. But stay with it longer. It's not a new set of clothes. Prayer will move us to the primary level, where we find out *what we really desire*: It's always God. It's always union, love, and communion. "Our hearts are restless until they rest in God," is how Saint Augustine (354–430) put it.[27] The sad thing about those who refuse to accept that state of longing and thirsting is that they are never satisfied anyway. Even the wealthiest person is never satisfied. The very character of greed is that it is insatiable. It needs an ever-higher dosage to achieve the old satisfaction. When we get more, it still doesn't satisfy. Jesus says, "Why not go in the exact opposite direction? Directly and positively choose emptiness until it loses its terror."

In all my years as a Catholic priest hearing confessions, I've never had anybody confess to violating the Tenth Commandment: coveting their neighbor's goods. Yet coveting goods forms the foundation of our entire culture. Billboards and advertisements create desire after desire.

Sales—the creating of false need through advertising and marketing—is the only game in town. I've also never had an American Christian seriously question the goal of increasing or maximizing profits.

When I first preached in the former Communist world, in eastern Germany, the most striking thing for me was to be in a world without any billboards or other advertisements. I didn't realize how much we're surrounded by them. A newspaper without a single advertisement is incredibly shorter than the papers to which we are accustomed. We don't realize how much our world is controlled by manufactured desires for things we do not need or really want. To quote Paul in a new context, "Who will rescue me from this body doomed to death?" (Romans 7:24b).

I have two practical suggestions that friends have shared with me for overcoming covetousness. One friend simply refuses to read or even look at *any* magazine or newspaper advertisements, even to check for sales or better prices. It only keeps us preoccupied with the whole game. Let's fast from advertising!

Another friend told me that when he found himself upset because he had been ripped off, lost money, made a bad financial choice, or the like, he developed the policy of giving that very amount he lost to charity. You could call it reverse double-dipping. I needed for him to repeat the idea to me because my save-a-penny attitude went into shock. That's probably how Jesus' hearers responded to him too.

"Blessed are the merciful: They shall have mercy shown them."
(Matthew 5:7)
Mercy is like the mystery of forgiveness. By definition, mercy and forgiveness are unearned, undeserved, not owed. If it isn't all three, it won't be experienced as mercy. If we think people *have* to be merciful, or, on the other hand, try to earn mercy, we have lost the mystery of mercy and forgiveness. *I believe with all my heart that mercy and forgiveness are the whole Gospel.*

The Benedictus (Luke 1:68–79) states we will have knowledge of salvation through the forgiveness of sin (1:77). The experience of forgiveness or mercy is the experience of a magnanimous God who loves out of total gratuitousness. There's no tit for tat, no buying and selling in the Temple (see Matthew 21:12). That is the symbolism of Jesus kicking over the tables: The buying and selling of God is over. We cannot buy and sell God by worthiness, by achievement, by obeying commandments. Salvation is God's lovingkindness, a lovingkindness that is *forever*. Read Psalm 136 for an ecstatic description.

We don't know mercy until we have really needed it. As Thomas Merton (1915–1968) once wrote—and I quoted it in chapter six: "Mercy within mercy within mercy." It's as if we collapse into deeper nets of acceptance, deeper nets of being enclosed, and finally find we're in a net out of which we can't fall. We are captured by grace. Only after much mistrust and testing do we accept that we are accepted.

I once saw God's mercy as patient, benevolent tolerance, a kind of grudging forgiveness. But now, mercy has become for me God's very self-understanding, a loving allowing, a willing breaking of the rules by the One who made the rules—a wink and a smile, a firm and joyful taking of our hand while we clutch at our sins and gaze at God in desire and disbelief. So many things have now become signs for me of this abundant mercy, not grudgingly extended, but patiently offered—to this church, to this age, to each of us. As we grow older, it almost takes more and more humility to receive the mercy of God.

Mercy is a way to describe the mystery of forgiveness. More than a description of something God does now and then, it is *who God is*. According to Jesus, "Mercy is what pleases me, not sacrifice" (Matthew 9:13, 12:7). The word is *hesed* in Hebrew, "the steadfast, enduring love which is unbreakable." Sometimes the word is translated as "lovingkindness" or "covenant love." God has made a covenant with creation and will never break the divine side of the covenant. It's only broken from our side. God's love is steadfast. It is written in the divine image within us. It's given. It sits there. We are the ones who clutch at our sins and beat ourselves instead of surrendering to the divine mercy. That refusal to be forgiven is a form of pride. It is saying, "I'm better than mercy. I'm only going to accept it when I'm worthy and can preserve my so-called self-esteem." Only the humble person, the little one, can live *in* and *after* mercy.

The mystery of forgiveness is God's ultimate entry into powerlessness. Look at the times when you have withheld forgiveness. It's always your final attempt to hold a claim over the one you won't forgive. It's the way we finally hold onto power, or seek the moral high ground over another person. "I will hold you in unforgiveness, and you're going to know it just by my coldness, by my not looking over there, by my refusal to smile." We do it subtly, to maintain our sense of superiority. Non-forgiveness is a form of power over another person, a way to manipulate, shame, control, and diminish another. God in Jesus refuses all such power.

If Jesus is the revelation of what is going on inside the eternal God (see Colossians 1:15), which is the core of Christian faith, then we are forced to conclude that God is very humble. That is amazing, and difficult to imagine. Sometimes I think I could just stop and meditate on that for the rest of my life. This God seems never to hold rightful claims against us. Abdicating what we thought was the proper role of God, this God "has thrust all my sins behind God's back" (see Isaiah 38:17b).

We do not attain anything by our own holiness, but by ten thousand surrenders to mercy. A lifetime of received forgiveness allows us to *become* mercy. That's the Beatitude. We become forgiveness because it's the only thing that makes sense to us, the only thing that's alive within us. Mercy becomes our energy, our meaning. Perhaps we are finally enlightened and free when we can both receive it and give it away—without payment or punishment.

Meditate, if you will, on this frontispiece I wrote for my book *Near Occasions of Grace.*

When grace is a punishment for you, you are in Hell.

When grace and punishment are fighting within you, you are in Purgatory.

When grace is received without payment or punishment, you are in Heaven.[28]

"Blessed are the pure in heart: They shall see God." (Matthew 5:8)

When the heart is right, seeing will be right, Jesus says. He ties together heart and sight. Consider the saying, "Beauty is in the eye of the beholder." So is God. All we need to do is keep the lens clean. If our heart is cold, our vision is distorted. Perhaps we don't like someone; we want to hurt her because she hurt us. We want to make him feel bad, to let him know that he hurt us. If we hold coldness and unforgiveness, or the desire to do violence verbally, or just to avert our loving gaze so that another person will feel our rejection, we will not be able to see clearly. Our heart is not pure.

Jesus says, "The lamp of your body is your eye. When your eye is clear, your whole body is also filled with light; but when it is diseased, your body also will be darkened" (Luke 11:34). What we always see in people who love God and themselves is the ability to make eye contact. When we hate ourselves, we cannot look someone else in the eye. People who do not know God or love will hate themselves and doubt the divine image within themselves. They shut us out, perhaps because they are afraid we will not see it there, either.

In my work as a jail chaplain, I found that the hardest thing to get the inmates to do was look at me eyeball to eyeball. They always put their heads down. There seemed to be a terrible sense of failure and inferiority. I wanted to hold up their heads sometimes and say, "Look at me. Don't you know you're a son of God, a beloved daughter?" But they closed their eyelids, as if to say, "Just don't look in here." There's too much power in the eye, too much power given and received. It might heal, it might change us, we might have to believe it. Truth comes through the eyes. It's very hard to lie with your eyes.

So, Jesus calls us to purity of heart with the promise that correct seeing will follow. In other places, he also says the opposite is true: Pure seeing will give us bright hearts.

"Blessed are the peacemakers: They shall be recognized as children of God." (Matthew 5:9)

This is the only time the word *peacemakers* is ever used in the whole Bible. A peacemaker literally is the "one who reconciles quarrels." We can clearly see Jesus is not on the side of the violent, but on the side of the nonviolent. Jesus is saying there must be a connection, a clear consistency, a constant unity between means and ends. There is no way to peace other than peacemaking itself.

Today, many think we can achieve peace through violence. Have you ever heard people say, "We will stop killing by killing"? Of course you have. It's the way we think, but it is in opposition to all great religious teachings. Our need for immediate control leads us to disconnect the clear unity between means and ends. We even named a missile that is clearly meant for the destruction of humanity a "peacekeeper." At least the word is more honest: peace*keeper*, instead of Jesus' peace*maker*. But the peace we are keeping is a false peace. Jeremiah the prophet would say about our "peacekeeping" wars what he said to the leaders of Israel:

"Peace! Peace!"
whereas there is no peace.
They should be ashamed of their loathsome deeds.
Not they! They feel no shame, they do not even know how to blush. (Jeremiah 8:11b–12a)

American Christians supported the killing of two hundred thousand people in Iraq during the Persian Gulf War and still dare to call themselves pro-life.

War is a means of seeking *control,* not a means of seeking peace. *Pax Romana* is the world's way of seeking control and calling it peace. In the ancient city of Rome, all the Romans thought they had peace. Everything seemed OK. Violence, you see, will always create more violence, but it creates the violence at the edge, out in the colonies. It calls what it has at the center "peace," yet the violence has merely been exported to the edges. It is not real peace. Our rich suburban enclaves with security entrances are evidence of the same today. As Paul VI (1897–1978) declared, "If you want peace, work for justice."[29]

Do we have any idea of all the slavery and oppression, all the killing and torture, all the millions of people who have lived in violence around the edges of every empire so those at the center of the empire could say they had peace? Every time you build a pyramid, certain people at the top will have their peace. Yet there will be bloody bodies all around the bottom. Those at the top are usually blind to the price of their false peace.

But in the Sermon, Jesus defines peace in a different way. We call this the *Pax Christi,* the peace of Christ. In the remaining Beatitudes, Jesus will connect his peace with justice and self-sacrifice. The *Pax Romana* creates a false peace by sacrificing others; the *Pax Christi* waits and works for true peace by sacrificing the false self of power, prestige, and possessions. That will never become the national policy of any country. It is unlikely to be espoused by any political party of any country at any time. Neither will such peacemaking ever be popular. The follower of Jesus is doomed to perennial minority status.

Jesus next warns us that we will be hated from all sides (see also John 15:18–16:2 or Matthew 10:22). When we are working for peace outside the system, we will not be admired inside the system. In fact, we will look dangerous, subversive, and unpatriotic through the lens of other people's fears. They used to call us Communists; now they're calling us Socialists. One thing we cannot call Jesus is a patriot. He was naming a far bigger world.

If we are truly pro-life, our very means have to be nonviolent and we have to be consistently pro-life—from womb to tomb. One of the most distressing qualities of Christians today is that they retain the right to decide when, where, and with whom they will be pro-life peacemakers. At the extreme end, if the other can be determined to be wrong, guilty, unworthy, sinful, or "not innocent" in any way, it is apparently acceptable to kill them. That entirely misses the ethical point that Jesus is making: We are *never* the sole arbiters of life or death, because life is created by God and carries the divine image. Why can't so-called conservatives and fundamentalists be strict about that?! It is a *spiritual seeing*, far beyond any ideology of left, right, or even church.

Each year, on the feast of John the Baptist, some of my coworkers and I would take a vow of nonviolence. We knew that we would never fully live up to it. Like any vow, it has to first find a home in the heart so that eventually we can live it in the outer world.

"Blessed are those who are persecuted in the cause of justice: The Reign of Heaven is theirs." (Matthew 5:10)

We should not be surprised that this Beatitude follows the previous ones. The first and the last Beatitudes are present tense: Theirs *is* the Reign of Heaven. Also, up until now, Jesus has said "happy are the," talking generally about groups. Now he says, "happy are those of *you*." Very likely, he's talking about what's going on right in front of him. Persecution has begun to happen to the believing community, and he's telling them to "rejoice and be glad"! Persecution for the cause of justice is inevitable. Instead of seeking to blame someone for their well-earned scars, he is telling them two clear things: You can be *happy*—*now*! Try living *that* in a country of lawyers and litigation.

I cannot help but wonder if an action that was motivated by conscience or the Gospel could ever be vindicated by whining, blaming, or suing. Perhaps all our lawsuits are, in fact, a recognition that the self we are defending is very fragile, insecure, and afraid.

The self that Jesus proclaims is so grounded that it can consider persecution an asset.

"Rejoice and be glad." (Matthew 5:12a)

Matthew 5:11–12 could really be called the ninth Beatitude, although it more likely is an explanation of the eighth:

> Blessed are you when people abuse you and persecute you and
> speak all kinds of calumny against you falsely on my account.
> Rejoice and be glad, for your reward will be great in heaven; this
> is how they persecuted the prophets before you.

Apparently, Jesus is saying that the disciples' response is a *prophetic* action in itself. To live joyfully in the midst of misunderstanding and persecution points beyond, to The Story. Jesus promises us that when we do live joyfully under persecution, the world won't understand. It will hate us. Many before me have said that a clear sign that something *is* true Gospel is if it engenders criticism and the spreading of falsehoods ("calumny"). Goodness can never be attacked directly; the messengers or the motivation have to be discredited.

Luke's Gospel presents the same message in exactly the opposite form: "Alas for you when the world speaks *well* of you! This was the way their ancestors treated the *false* prophets" (Luke 6:26, emphases added). Too much praise is probably an indication that it is *not* the full Gospel. In either case, Jesus himself clearly knew that his teaching would turn conventional values on their head.

Who Will Preserve the Essentials?

Jesus says that those who live these happinesses, these Beatitudes, will be "the salt of the earth" (see Matthew 5:13). What does he mean by such an image?

First of all, he's *not* saying that those who live this way are going to heaven. He is saying that they will be a certain kind of gift for the *earth*. What a misinterpretation has been handed on, again and again! We think of Jesus' teaching as a set of *prescriptions* for getting to heaven (even though we haven't followed them). No, the Sermon on the Mount and especially the Beatitudes are a set of *descriptions* of a free life. They are more than prescriptions, so don't even try to interpret them in the mode of law.

Jesus' moral teaching is very often a description of the final product rather than a detailed process for getting there. When we can weep, when we can identify with the little ones, when we can make peace, when we can be persecuted and still be joyful—then we are doing it right. He is saying, as it were, that this is what holiness will look like. When we act this way, "the Reign of God is among you" (Luke 17:21b). Jesus has low control needs, it seems. His concerns are proclamation, naming, revealing, stating. Then he trusts that good-willed people and a reliable God will take it from there. Jesus is not concerned about enforcement or uniformity. What a shame that we can't do the same.

"If salt becomes tasteless, how can we salt the world with it?" asks Jesus (see Matthew 5:13). That message seems especially true today. If we no longer believe the Gospel, if we no longer believe in nonviolence and powerlessness, then who's going to convert *us*? We're supposed to be the leaven of the world, yet if we no longer believe in the Gospel, what hope do we have of offering anything new to the nations?

It seems so many saints and prophets who start out to preach to the world come back to convert or reconvert the People of God. Until the church believes its own core message, there's no point in going out and telling other people to be Christian. There is no new world order to point to or to bring them home to. Jesus' conclusion is rather pessimistic compared to our practice of plugging along with an awful lot of "salt that has lost its zing." He says, "It's good for nothing but to be thrown out and trampled underfoot." Wow!

By calling his disciples "salt of the earth," he's not saying they're the saved ones. He never tries to create a "members-only" club. Jesus consistently says, in fact, that God loves those on the outside just as much as God loves the insiders; that there's just as much mercy *out* there as *in* here among Jesus' closest followers. If we don't believe our own message, we're good for nothing. We do more harm than good.

Jesus is calling us to creative self-criticism and giving us the capacity for self-regeneration. As long as some people hold on to the upside-down wisdom of the Gospel, it will be enough to flavor the whole meal of life. The Good News gives a taste to the world.

In short, it is not as important that each individual "gets saved" as it is that the Gospel wisdom be in the world for *our* salvation. Western individualists have a hard time with that. Salt is tiny and even invisible when it dissolves, but for ancient people it was the only preservative, the only spice, and often a symbol of healing.

Just Do It Better

Finally, Jesus says, "You are light for the world. A city built on a hilltop cannot be hidden" (Matthew 5:14). We used to say in the seminary, "That which is tottering need not be pushed." It's not real, and it's going to fall apart anyway, so why waste your time getting mad at it? Why waste your time attacking it? Conversely, Jesus is saying here that the real cannot be destroyed—only ignored. The unreal will show itself as unreal in time. Our job is to be a shining truth, to live on the mountaintop, to live the truth as best we can and let things fall where they may. What a difficult and non-pushy way to live! "The best criticism of the bad is the practice of the better" has become a near-motto for me and one of the eight core principles of our work at the Center for Action and Contemplation.

"In the same way your light must shine in people's sight, so that, seeing your good works, they may give praise to your Father in heaven" (Matthew 5:16). Jesus says "*your* Father" as a calm and secure assumption. He is seemingly trying to invite us into the same relationship with God that he has. "He's not just *my* Father," Jesus is saying, "but he's also yours." So, we needn't be the mountaintop, the city, the whole house. We're simply that which shines on the mountaintop, which illuminates the house. We're not the whole loaf of bread, we're just the leaven. We're not the whole meal—we're not the broccoli, mashed potatoes, or roast beef; we're just the salt, and our shared and loving God is the banquet, the mountain, and the focus of all praise.

What modest images these are. I don't think Jesus ever expected the whole world to follow him. Obviously, the world is not all going to become Christian. For the most part, the only people who are being converted to Christianity today are secular types and animists. Muslims, Hindus, Jews, and Buddhists seldom become Christians. The cultural barriers are too vast. Jesus is telling his disciples, "I've given you a great truth. I want you to hold the light and the leaven in the middle of the world. As light or leaven, it will do its work, and God's purposes will be achieved." What relaxed and patient trust Jesus has in God!

Although his images are very modest, they are also very hopeful. The church has always been the most effective, I think, when it has been in a minority or even persecuted position. The Spirit works best underground, when we work from the bottom. Jesus surely never intended Christendom to be Gospel imposed by law, government, and majority status. God knows we've tried, but as soon as the church became establishment, as soon as we came into power, we lost the true power, the effective virus of the Gospel. Jesus says we are a mere mustard seed, we are leaven, we are the pearl of great price, we are a hidden treasure in the field.

Jesus is quite content, it seems, with such a humble position. He always enters the imperial city from a place of powerlessness. Our path, apparently, must be the same: "Do not be afraid, daughter of Zion; see, your king is coming, mounted on a colt of a donkey" (see Zechariah 9:9).

The introductory teaching in the Sermon on the Mount has to do with a new understanding and strategy of power. Jesus is leading us into the power that is apparently the power of God. To us, it feels like powerlessness.

chapter nine

Bridges and Boundaries:
Liberals and Conservatives

Do not imagine that I have come to abolish the Law or the Prophets. I have come not to abolish but to complete them. In truth I tell you, till heaven and earth disappear, not one dot, not one little stroke, is to disappear from the Law until all its purpose is achieved. Therefore, anyone who infringes even one of the least of these commandments and teaches others to do the same will be considered the least in the Reign of Heaven; but the person who keeps them and teaches them will be considered great in the Reign of Heaven. (Matthew 5:17–19)

Notice how Jesus now leads into his teaching on the Law: "I have not come to abolish the Law" (Cool it, liberals!); the Law will not disappear "until its purpose is achieved" (Beware, mindless legalists!); "Your virtue must go deeper than the scribes and Pharisees or you will never enter the Reign of Heaven" (It's about God's values and depth, not just external behavior).

Here we have the balance Jesus strikes between what we call conservative and liberal. He holds onto the foundation and center of the old, while moving the boundaries out much farther than almost anyone expected. On a continuum between inclusiveness and exclusiveness, we see that

Jesus is trying to find a delicate balance. Exclusivity at its extreme would have been the Law of Holiness (Leviticus chapters 17–25). Such an exclusive approach to Law can mean petrification, solidification, isolation, and irrelevance. That's true in any group when boundaries between insiders and outsiders become overemphasized. But it also gives a group a strong and often psychologically healthy sense of identity and boundaries. We surely could use that today.

But inclusivity at its extreme, where all the boundaries are thrown out and "everything is beautiful," as the liberal type wants to say, very often can mean standing for nothing, betrayal of central and essential truths. That can eventually lead to disintegration of the group. Nothing enduring can be built when there's a refusal to stand for anything. After a while, we ask the question, "Well, why belong?" It doesn't really matter because there's no real group identity. So, liberals generally don't build anything enduring. Wisdom is knowing how to hold both inclusion and exclusion in ideal tension. We're going to see that Jesus is really a master at that.

Charles Williams (1886–1945), a brilliant Christian writer, described this tension very well. He wrote that "the rigorous view," what I am calling exclusivity, "is vital to sanctity; the relaxed view is vital to sanctity. Their union is not impossible, but it is difficult; for whichever is in power begins, after the first five minutes, to maintain itself from bad and unworthy motives. Harshness, pride, resentment encourage the one; indulgence, falsity, detestable good-fellowship the other."[30]

On the side of exclusivity, we might hear, "We are the true people who have got it." Williams' description of the possible sin on the other end is even more interesting: this need to feel good that often characterizes the liberal. On the side of inclusivity, we might hear, "There are no real boundaries for which I need to stand because the all-important thing is that you like me and I like you." Abdication never leads to depth or integrity. If we don't believe in anything, we will fall for everything.

Williams is daring enough to state something that we probably wouldn't say today: "detestable good-fellowship." But I get the point. If we're willing to betray the deeper self to feel good and manufacture cheap communion in the moment, in the long run we don't have anything enduring. Williams later concludes, "Our Lord the Spirit is reluctant to allow either of the two great ways [the rigorous way or the relaxed way] to flourish without some courtesy to the other."[31] It reminds me of what I often say in spiritual direction to the more rigorous types, to those who are trying too hard to maintain self-image in one direction. I say, "Make sure you nod to your shadow each day." In other words, give yourself some gentle recognition that you are also lazy, ordinary, sensual—whatever it might be—because when you repress the shadow too rigorously, it will always come out indirectly anyway. Everybody else can see it but you.

Further on, Jesus talks about not seeing the great log in our own eye, yet seeing the splinter in somebody else's (see Matthew 7:4). That, I think, is a marvelous description of the shadow. We must recognize the dark side within ourselves. That leads us to the relaxed view. Once we see that what we hate *over there* is largely a projection of what's *in here*, an attempt to maintain ourselves in superiority, then we can't be overly rigorous. Rigorism usually is tied up with a strong ability to repress what we don't want to see: the dark side.

On the other hand, the relaxed view sins not by repression, but by too-quick *expression*. At both extremes, we lose the energy that teaches. Too-quick expression, too-quick consummation loses the real power of the moment, the creative insight, because we act on it before we have learned its lessons. That's really the meaning of celibacy too. Healthy celibates learn how to live their loneliness until their erotic longings become the ultimate longing: the longing for God. It's the same with patience itself, poverty, silence, fasting, forgiveness, letting go, and nonviolence.

The modern philosophy, "If it feels good, do it," is just as useless to the soul as repression. Extreme repression and extreme expression are both evidence of people who aren't going to grow up. They aren't going to learn very much from their experience. We are called to live in the middle, where we live with the energy for a while—the temptation, the experience, the moment—and let it teach us, even at the cost of pain. Repression is the means of control; expression is the means of avoiding control. Truth lies somewhere in between—the rightly called "golden mean" or *via media*.

In that in-between place, we've got to build a bridge between power and powerlessness. Jesus taught us that we start on the side of powerlessness, but that doesn't make power wrong. Ultimately, we have to learn how to use power creatively. One word for the Holy Spirit is *dynamos*, which means "power." The only people who can be trusted with power are those who know how to live creatively with powerlessness. Liberals tend to hate or mistrust power. Conservatives tend to fear or avoid powerlessness.

The only people whom I can trust with saying, "It's important to be Catholic," for example, are those who know that Catholic isn't finally what it's all about. The Reign of God is what it's all about. Once we are committed to those values, we can rightly pull back into a *healthy* exclusivity. We need a solid ground, an Archimedean point, from which we can move the world. I don't suppose there is any other way—at least, I don't know of any, historically. It is a marvelous balancing act for which few will take responsibility today. Jesus seems to have achieved the human patience, the unwillingness to hurt or react, the critical intelligence, and the urgent love that come together to create that rare thing called wisdom.

Transforming Initiatives

After the prefatory remarks that challenge both ends of the ideological spectrum (Matthew 5:17–20), Jesus now moves into his concrete analysis of the Mosaic Law. This reinterpretation has been written off by most of the church as high-minded idealism. We don't really take it seriously because in our world order, it is not realistic. If we took it seriously at all, we would be encouraged to interpret it in terms of private morality, but not in terms of an institution, a group, a family—certainly not our nation-states. States can't possibly be encouraged to love their enemies or we'd have no world order, right?

Yet a scholar named Glen Stassen (1936–2014) pointed out that what we have here, in just fourteen verses beginning at Matthew 5:21, is not simply high-minded idealism, but a concrete plan for deliverance from vicious cycles.[32] Each paragraph first states traditional piety, conventional religion, then what Stassen calls the mechanism of bondage or vicious cycle. Jesus' insight is that each good law—obeyed *apart from the Spirit*—carries with it a way to entrap us. (Isn't that exactly what Paul concludes in both Romans and Galatians?) After naming the mechanism of bondage, Jesus names the flip side: a transforming initiative. The term *triad*—a name for a musical chord of three interrelated tones—captures the unity of these three elements in each passage (see the following chart). This is the most helpful analysis of this section I have ever studied. It does not paralyze with idealism and force us to dismissal, nor does it back off from a very real initiative that we can take.

The Fourteen Triads of the Sermon on the Mount

Matthew 5:21–7:11

The traditional challenge of a religious culture	But, the problem is:	The Way of Transformation
1. You shall not kill.	You still nurse anger and accusation.	Go, be reconciled first.
2. You shall not commit adultery.	Fantasy and lustful looking continue.	Way of seeing demands radical surgery.

The traditional challenge of a religious culture	But, the problem is:	The Way of Transformation
3. Men may divorce by writ of dismissal.	This is one-sided adultery.	Call to equality in dialogue seems to have been forgotten.
4. Do not take oaths.	Legal swearing only binds you into loyalty systems and mistrust.	Keep your language very simple and personal.
5. "Eye for eye" morality as justice.	De facto vengeance and violent resistance.	You change the rules of the game: "turn cheek," etc.
6. Love "family" and ignore/"hate" others.	This gets us nowhere and keeps our love small.	Love the outsider and practice by praying for them.
Re-emphasized by: Show recognition to those like you.	Everybody does that; not really love or virtue.	*GOD IMITATION: total inclusivity.*
7. Give alms to the poor.	Keeps religion on level of externals and observance. Maintains your morally superior image.	Do it secretly to avoid any public or personal payoff.
8. Pray.	Be wary of the perks of social prayer.	Contemplative prayer of quiet: behind door and no payoff.
9. More and better prayer will talk God into it.	This maintains you in a false relationship and image of God.	OUR FATHER names the relationship and world rightly.

The traditional challenge of a religious culture	But, the problem is:	The Way of Transformation
10. Fast (necessary call to under-stimulation, detachment, simplifying).	Dour, dismal, and overly serious religious people.	Keep it light, happy, and smiling; do it for truth, not payoff.
11. Don't consume and hoard.	Greed never satisfies, and you lose it anyway.	Spiritual investment lasts. Do it!
12. Can't serve both God and the system ("mammon.")	You still remain divided, enslaved, and preoccupied.	It's not about the "hot sins" but anxiety about the daily things. "Stop worrying" repeated five times.
13. Do not judge.	Because it becomes the whole way you see reality and even your-self. Gives you a false sense of control and not truth or love.	Shadow denial leads to shadow projection. See yourself in others and *forgive it over there* to stop the cycle.
14. "Don't throw pearls before swine," etc.	Unready people only misunderstand and turn against you.	Ask, search, know, pray, wait. God will give "good things" in time.

Let's go through each of the triads:

1. You have heard how it was said to our ancestors, *You shall not kill*; and if anyone does kill, they must answer for it before the court. But I say this to you: Anyone who is angry with a brother or sister will answer for it before the court, anyone who calls a brother or sister "Fool" will answer for it before the Sanhedrin, and anyone who calls them "Traitor" will answer for it in hellfire.

So then, if you are bringing your offering to the altar and there remember that your brother or sister has something against you, leave your offering there before the altar, go and be reconciled with them first, and then come back and present your offering. Come to terms with your opponent in good time, while you are still on the way to the court with them, or they may hand you over to the judge and the judge to the officer, and you will be thrown into prison. In truth I tell you, you will not get out until you have paid the last penny. (Matthew 5:21–26)

The first sentence of this initiative is traditional religion. Who would disagree with it? But nursing anger is the mechanism of bondage. To nurse anger—for example, to call another person a fool and hold ill will against that person—will get us just as trapped as killing and will finally lead us to killing. Therefore, the transforming initiative: Go and be reconciled while there's still time, before we can nurse anger in our heart and build up hatred toward another person.

2. You have heard how it was said, *You shall not commit adultery.* But I say this to you: If a man looks at a woman lustfully, he has already committed adultery with her in his heart. If your right eye should be your downfall, tear it out and throw it away, for it will do you less harm to lose one part of yourself than to have your whole body thrown into hell. And if your right hand should be your downfall, cut it off and throw it away, for it will do you less harm to lose one part of yourself than to have your whole body go to hell. (Matthew 5:27–30)

Of course we must not commit adultery, but Jesus always goes one step deeper. The real mechanism of bondage is to look at another person as an object (with lust, as it says in the text). To commit adultery in the heart, to try to make another person an object for our consumption: that's the mechanism of bondage.

What is Jesus' transforming initiative? Remove even the cause of the temptation. Stop playing the whole mind-game called fantasy. His teaching images of tearing out eyes and cutting off hands are an indication of how hard he knew it would be to discipline mind, heart, and senses. It has nothing to do with the real world of relationship. That's the real sin: creating relationships in our heads. Relationships don't happen in the head; they happen in the real world. See how radical Jesus is? He always deals with causes, not symptoms. (A radical is one who gets to the *radix*, the root of things. That's neither a bad idea nor a negative criticism.)

> 3. It has also been said, *Anyone who divorces his wife must give her a writ of dismissal.* But I say this to you: Everyone who divorces his wife, except for the case of an illicit marriage, makes her an adulteress; and anyone who marries a divorced woman commits adultery. (Matthew 5:31–32)

The primary point of Jesus' teaching on divorce is to bring back equality between men and women, not to declare eternal indissolubility (the latter interpretation is a good example of how sexism kept us from reading the exact meaning of the text). Divorce was allowed in Jewish culture, but totally from the side of the male. He had all the power. If he didn't like his wife's looks, he could declare one day that they were divorced. What Jesus is doing, again, is taking the side of the oppressed—in this case, the side of the female—and saying, "You men can't keep having it your way." It's an equal system and *both parties* must have the right to take the initiative. Justice and truth must be done between you, and *both* must take responsibility for the death of a marriage, which Matthew 5:32 seems to recognize will sometimes happen.

The mechanism of bondage is precisely one-sidedness, which destroys any real meaning of possible reconciliation, dialogue, or basic justice. The transforming initiative is to create a *true partnership* and work from there. That's revolutionary teaching!

4. Again, you have heard how it was said to our ancestors, *You must not break your oath, but must fulfill your oaths to the Lord.* But I say this to you: Do not swear at all, either by heaven, since that is God's throne; or by earth, since that is God's footstool; or by Jerusalem, since that is the city of the great king. Do not swear by your own head either, since you cannot turn a single hair white or black. All you need to say is "Yes" if you mean yes, "No" if you mean no. Anything more than this comes from the Evil One. (Matthew 5:33–37)

The mechanism of bondage in this case is that swearing by anything involves us with evil and with judgment. Remember, the system up through the feudal age was held together by the taking of oaths (see chapter four). We don't understand it so much because we don't understand the patron/client world of that prior era.

This, by the way, is an example of how some things are taken from the teaching of Jesus and made into absolute commandments, while other things are completely ignored. We're going to get the last bit of blood out of Jesus' injunction about adultery, but the very next injunction on taking oaths has been, for the most part, ignored. Jesus says, "Don't promise your loyalty to any system." But do you know a single Christian who was ever kicked out of a church for taking an oath? There are only a few sects that take this seriously. It's strange that we would perhaps consider the Amish to be sectarian, when their interpretation of the ban on oath-taking is likely correct and consistent.

"Let your yes be yes, and your no be no," is Jesus' transforming initiative. Can we live in such a world, where we talk to one another with absolute, simple truth and our word is good? Allow me to repeat an example I've used elsewhere: My father ran a gas station in western Kansas. He used to speak of the hard times around the Great Depression. Many people couldn't pay for even five gallons of gas. He'd always just say, "When you can pay it, pay it." As he recalled, almost all of them finally paid. He said that once someone came back and gave him a ten-dollar bill for the gas ten years later.

I know we can't go back to such a world. I'm sure, if you went to your local gas station and told them you'd pay them later, they wouldn't give you any gas. But Jesus is taking the initiative about a new world order, where people's word can mean something with one another.

A world of oaths, swearing, and suing (as we have today) is founded on mistrust, impersonalism, and lack of relationship. That is the old world order, and yet even we Christians expect truth and justice from it. We go to Caesar for what Christ has already offered us—but what we didn't accept from him.

Interestingly, Saint Francis, in his Rule for the Third Order, required that laypeople neither possess "lethal weapons" nor take oaths, "except for peace, for the Faith, under calumny, and in bearing witness."[33] Recent historians have credited the widely followed Rule with partial responsibility for the fall of the entire feudal system of nobility and serfdom! Without arms and oaths of loyalty, it could not stand. Did Jesus not have the same intention for the yeast that he was offering to civilization in these seemingly innocuous admonitions?

> 5. You have heard how it was said: *Eye for eye and tooth for tooth.* But I say this to you: Offer no resistance to the wicked. On the contrary, if anyone hits you on the right cheek, offer them the other as well. If someone wishes to go to law with you to get your tunic, let them have your cloak as well. And if anyone requires you to go one mile, go two miles with them. Give to anyone who asks you, and if anyone wants to borrow, do not turn away. (Matthew 5:38–42)

The mechanism of bondage here is violent resistance. The whole problem is in the inner attitude. Jesus' great transforming initiative is, "Turn the other cheek: Let them have your clothes as well. Why even play the game? If someone asks you to go one mile, go two with them." In Jesus' time, a conscripted soldier was allowed to ask any person to carry his armor for one mile. That's the image upon which Jesus is building. He's saying, "Just don't get into the tit-for-tat game; carry it two miles. Create your own loving set of rules, which will blow the system apart. *You* take the initiative and change the rules, the expectations, and the outcome."

> 6. You have heard how it was said: *You will love your neighbor* and hate your enemy. But I say this to you: Love your enemies and pray for those who persecute you, so that you may be children of your Father in heaven, for God causes the sun to rise on the bad as well as the good, and sends down rain to fall on the upright and the wicked alike. For if you love those who love you, what reward will you get? Do not even the tax collectors do as much? (Matthew 5:43–46)

Traditional piety tells us to love our neighbor, love the in-group. Loving and greeting only those who love us, Jesus says, is simply a mechanism of bondage. It's keeping us in a small world of warm fuzzies, but actually inoculating us from the often dark and daring world of real love. It actually protects and perpetuates the world of scapegoats, victimization, and projection.

This sixth triad is considered the most radical, demanding, and truthful of all of Jesus' teaching. Until there is love for enemies, there is no real transformation, because the enemy always carries the dark side of our own soul. Normally, those people who threaten us carry our own faults in a different form. The people who really turn us off are very much like us. Jesus offers this not just as a suggestion; we have *got* to love our enemy to grow up. Jesus rightly puts it in the imperative form: *Do* it!

Also, what we don't like about ourselves is our inner enemy, in a certain sense. We must learn to love and forgive that enemy too. Sometimes that takes great humility and great compassion, but if we learn it internally, we will be prepared for the outer enemies.

> And if you save your greetings for your brothers and sisters, are you doing anything exceptional? Do not even the gentiles do as much? You must therefore set no bounds to your love, just as your heavenly Father sets none to his. (Matthew 5:47–48)

This sixth triad is one long but dramatic idea: If you greet only your brother or sister, what's so great about that? The ultimately alienating process is that if you stay inside your religious/ethnic group, wars and racism continue. That's just staying inside a kind of magnified self-love. The key is always to love the stranger at the gate. Love the one outside of your comfort zone, the outsider, the other. "Until you can enter into the experience of the outsider and the other," Jesus says, "you really have not loved at all." What's his motivation for doing this? The all-inclusiveness of the Father.

What Jesus suggests is a kind of *imitatio Deo*, an imitation of God. If that's who God is and that's the way God loves, then that's how we want to love. God rubs off on people who hang around God. If God "sets no bounds," then we have to stop keeping score and weighing worthiness.

The final imperative is well translated here by *The New Jerusalem Bible*. The common translation, "be perfect" (*teleios*), is a later abstract Greek concept Jesus would never have used. He spoke in concrete and descriptive Aramaic metaphors, never like a cerebral philosopher or even a theologian. He is, however, admitting that this most demanding commandment is going to ask a great deal of us—boundlessness and magnanimity.

> 7. So, when you give alms, do not have it trumpeted before you; this is what the hypocrites do in the synagogues and in the streets to win human admiration. In truth I tell you, they have had their reward. But when you give alms, your left hand should

> not know what your right is doing. Your almsgiving must be
> secret, and your Father who sees all that is done in secret will
> reward you. (Matthew 6:2–4)

Giving alms is traditional piety. The mechanism of bondage is doing religious practices in public and getting hung up on what people think about us. Religion's perennial temptation is to get trapped *in persona*. Externalization is always the avoidance of true relationship and communion. The transforming initiative is: Don't do it out loud, do it secretly.

Remember what I noted in chapter four about an honor/shame culture. Jesus is trying to get his people to own their identity and motivation from within. He is trying to get them out of the hall of mirrors, the world of imitation and spiritual competition that keeps people shallow and essentially insecure. "Don't let your left hand know what your right hand is doing—just *act* and forget about the rewards or fruits of your action." Act for the truth of the action itself and not for human approval or the flattering self-image. That is radical surgery.

> 8. And when you pray, do not imitate the hypocrites. They love
> to say their prayers standing up in the synagogues and at the
> street corners for people to see them. In truth I tell you, they
> have had their reward. But when you pray, go to your private
> room, shut yourself in, and so pray to your Father who is in that
> secret place, and your Father who sees all that is done in secret
> will reward you. (Matthew 6:5–6)

The mechanism of bondage is doing prayer in public; therefore, pray in secret. In today's terms, go in the closet, where you have no motivation except seeking the truth, seeking God, seeking love. Again, Jesus wants action for its own sake and not for some outer image or inner product.

This teaching is useful in contemplative training and for those who say Jesus never taught contemplation. In his Semitic, concrete style, he does speak of separation, quiet, and under-stimulation with the image of a closed closet door. He could also be interpreted as advising a prayer style that does not seem to have any immediate or social payoff. That's exactly what perseverance in contemplative prayer requires. We sometimes forget that Jesus was a mystic.

9. In your prayers, do not babble as the gentiles do, for they think that by using many words they will make themselves heard. Do not be like them. Your Father knows what you need before you ask. So, you should pray like this:

Our Father in heaven,
may your name be held holy,
your reign come,
your will be done,
on earth as in heaven.
Give us today our daily bread.
And forgive us our debts,
as we have forgiven those who are in debt to us.
And do not put us to the test,
but save us from the Evil One.

Yes, if you forgive others their failings, your heavenly Father will forgive you yours; but if you do not forgive others, your Father will not forgive your failings either. (Matthew 6:7–15)

A lot of us pray as if prayer is really twisting the arm of God or convincing God to do something. We think that by saying more words, we'll talk God into it. We think, "If I say it one more time, God will agree with me." That very attitude is an alienating attitude. It keeps us in the role of doing it "right" or often enough to convince an unready or unwilling God.

Instead, Jesus gives us seven simple statements of petition to *align* our prayer with the eternal and effective will of God (as opposed to placating an angry God or talking God into things God would rather not do).

This is Jesus' transforming initiative, an alternative to "babbling like the pagans." With an imperative, he says, "Pray like this," and presents the ideal spoken prayer.

> 10. When you are fasting, do not put on a gloomy look as the hypocrites do. They go about looking unsightly to let people know they are fasting. In truth I tell you, they have had their reward. But when you fast, put scent on your head and wash your face, so that no one will know you are fasting except your Father, who sees all that is done in secret, and your Father who sees all that is done in secret will reward you. (Matthew 6:16–18)

Along with the traditional piety of fasting comes a mechanism of bondage: walking around revealing the self as fasting and observant. The transforming initiative: Anoint your head, wash your face, forget about any public display of fasting. It has to be done quietly, within our own life and heart. Jesus is a master at breaking all "social contagion" that keeps humans interactive but utterly *ungrounded*. A certain degree of solitude and silence is the transforming mechanism in all three religious disciplines: prayer, almsgiving, and fasting. Prayer frees us for God, almsgiving frees us for others, and fasting frees us from ourselves.

> 11. Do not store up treasures for yourselves on earth, where moth and woodworm destroy them, and thieves can break in and steal. But store up treasures for yourselves in heaven, where neither moth nor woodworm destroys them, and thieves cannot break in and steal. For wherever your treasure is, there will your heart be too. (Matthew 6:19–21)

The alienating process is that consumerism finally lets us down anyway. It promises more than it can deliver. Get the lead on it by putting all your satisfaction somewhere else. Jesus uses the banking/investment image, but instead applies it to spiritual goods. As John Paul II (1920–2005) said to the United Nations, material goods decrease by usage, but spiritual goods actually increase when we make use of them.[34] It's all a Semitic way of saying, "What you love reveals who you are."

> 12. No one can be the slave of two masters. You will either hate the first and love the second, or be attached to the first and despise the second. You cannot be the slave both of God and of money.
>
> That is why I am telling you not to worry about your life and what you are to eat, nor about your body and what you are to wear. Surely life is more than food, and the body more than clothing! Look at the birds in the sky. They do not sow or reap or gather into barns; yet your heavenly Father feeds them. Are you not worth much more than they are? Can any of you, however much you worry, add one single cubit to your span of life? And why worry about clothing? Think of the flowers growing in the fields. They never have to work or spin, yet I assure you that not even Solomon in all his royal robes was clothed like one of these. Now, if that is how God clothes the wildflowers growing in the field, which are there today and thrown into the furnace tomorrow, will he not much more look after you, you who have so little faith? So do not worry. Do not say, "What are we to eat? What are we to drink? What are we to wear?" It is the gentiles who set their hearts on all these things. Your heavenly Father knows you need them all. Set your hearts on his Reign first, and on God's saving justice, and all these other things will be given to you as well. So do not worry about tomorrow; tomorrow will take care of itself. Each day has enough trouble of its own. (Matthew 6:24–34)

This oft-quoted passage speaks better than any commentary, but to illustrate the triad as Matthew carries it out: (1) The traditional religious practice is to have it both ways: love the system and still love God. (2) Jesus says it will prove impossible, that it will hold you bound. (3) The transforming initiative is not to be anxious (repeated in five ways) and, positively, to "set your heart on God's Reign and God's justice." That's classic Jesus teaching in summary and poetic form.

> 13. Do not judge and you will not be judged, because the judgments you give are the judgments you will get, and the standard you use will be the standard used for you. Why do you observe the splinter in your brother's eye and never notice the great log in your own? And how dare you say to your brother, "Let me take that splinter out of your eye," when, look, there is a great log in your own? Hypocrite! Take the log out of your own eye first, and then you will see clearly enough to take the splinter out of your brother's eye. (Matthew 7:1–5)

Why do you think Jesus tells us not to judge? First of all, judgment is very often a means of control, not a means of looking for the truth. It's a means of securing the self or undoing other people by categorizing them. Sometimes we hate and condemn ourselves in the same way. That type of judgment is not of God. Judging a person to be morally superior or morally inferior, right or wrong, good or bad seldom leads to deeper insight or compassion. It's another way of eating of the tree of knowledge of good and evil and gaining a false sense of security or moral high ground.

Yet there's another form of judgment that is absolutely necessary: choosing for ourselves between two options. "This is of value, this is not of value. This is what God is calling me to, this is not what God is calling me to." Call it discrimination or discernment, if you will. It is not only good, but a necessary and holy meaning of our English word *judgment*.

Because *judgment* in English has these two meanings, this has been a problematic passage for many people. We say, "Well, we've got to make judgments." True, but whenever we are doing it to control or to condemn ourselves or others, to explain or to justify or to validate ourselves or others, at that point we are not normally looking for truth, we're looking for control. That's the judgment Jesus is talking about in this passage. It's a form of entrapment to be avoided. Now we know that Jesus was far ahead of his time as a student of human nature. This particular passage is an excellent statement on self-hatred, denial of shadow, and necessary projection of denied shadow. Psychologist Carl Jung even referred to Jesus' excellent and transforming initiative: "Take the log out of your own eye" means the same as "own your own shadow."

14. Do not give dogs what is holy and do not throw your pearls in front of pigs, or they may trample them and then turn on you and tear you to pieces.

Ask, and it will be given to you; search, and you will find; knock, and the door will be opened to you. Everyone who asks receives, everyone who searches finds, and everyone who knocks will have the door opened. Is there anyone among you who would hand their son a stone when he asked for bread, or would hand him a snake when he asked for a fish? If you, then, evil as you are, know how to give your children what is good, how much more will your Father in heaven give good things to those who ask him! (Matthew 7:6–11)

There's no point in giving wisdom or truth to people who psychically and spiritually aren't ready for it. That may seem like a harsh statement to us, but it's utter realism. Sometimes when we offer truth too early, people write off the whole message because the heart or soul isn't ready for it yet. Then they are worse off than when we started.

I saw many people, for example, naïvely come to join communities in the early 1970s, when the community movement was strong. They really weren't coming for the right reasons. There was no real discernment. They were often avoiding home or wanting a belonging system. Their souls weren't ready for it. They were given a pearl of great price and truth, but they had no capacity for such truth. Many of these folks left community and now they speak despairingly of the "c-word." Some feel that pearls were "trampled on" by the very people who received the most, and moreover, "they turned on you and tore you to pieces." In this passage, Jesus sounds like he is speaking from experience.

Jesus understands timing, patience, and growth. His transforming initiative is to give the request to God in prayer: "Ask, and it will be given to you, search and you will find, and knock and the door will be opened to you" (Matthew 7:7). In other words, hold off; don't push the river. Don't demand blood from a turnip. Ask, search, knock. He moves the temptation to anger, blame, and self-pity to an entirely different framework. Don't waste time with shame and blame. Seek "good things"—bread, fish, and open doors—from a God who is apparently the Ultimate Parent.

When we wait, when we listen, when we "knock and ask," we find the real demons, the sources of bondage, the real things that are tying us up. They're usually not what they seem. I'm convinced a lot of anger today is grief. Some of today's fear is grief too.

Yet we can't build on fear *or* anger. We can't build on the negative. We only can build on faith, on freedom, on truth. If we build on fear, in the end, we will have a house of fear. To build on anger is not to build at all, for the anger will return to us in our families, our employees, and our own sour souls.

Many people derive lots of energy by being angry at the pope, bishops, priests, husbands, wives, or whomever else. In the end, it's a waste of time. Nothing is built. Jesus ends the Sermon on the Mount by contrasting the one who built a house on rock to the one who built on sand (see Matthew 7:24–27).

I never thought any of my words would end up on a T-shirt, but when I handed over the Center for Action and Contemplation in Albuquerque to lay leadership, they printed shirts. Of all my too-many words, they chose these for the back of one shirt: "We cannot build on death, we can only build on life. We must be sustained by a sense of what we are for and not just what we are against." That was the end of my sermon too, I guess.

The fourteen triads are then summed up in a transformative one-liner that perhaps sums up their entire momentum. No wonder we call it "the golden rule": "Always treat others as you would like them to treat you; that is the Law and the Prophets" (Matthew 7:12).

The Lord's Prayer

Let us go back into the Sermon and give special treatment to the Our Father, the Lord's Prayer, the prayer that Jesus taught us. Books, of course, have been written on it, but perhaps we can glean some insights in a few pages. When I was in hermitage many years ago, I spent a lot of time trying not only to study the Lord's Prayer, but also to pray it and understand it on a deeper level. This is what stayed with me.

First, the prayer aligns all relationships truthfully and situates us correctly in the universe if we just believe it and act out of it. Beginning with the first word, *our*, we are taught that we are social beings and that our relationship with God is not "mine" or private. We either come to God together or we don't come at all.

Second, a healthy sense of spirituality is a sense that God is simultaneously *transcendent* and *immanent*. It senses a God who dwells within—each of us is a temple of the Holy Spirit—but equally a God who is utterly beyond and before whom we can only bow down. The very first phrase of the Lord's Prayer keeps that perfectly in balance.

"*Our Father in heaven*" (Matthew 6:9b): God is the beloved *Abba*, the beloved parent who dwells within each of us and in whose image we are created. Yet this loving God, who does not accuse us, who does not shame us but, in fact, nurtures us and holds us, is also totally beyond us "in heaven." Contemporary spirituality and practice still seek that ideal synthesis. Most groups exaggerate one side or the other. Jesus names both as true.

"*May your name be held holy*" (Matthew 6:9c): Great religion is about adoration, about Someone before whom we bow. If we do not, we will soon bow before ourselves. If the center of the world is not out there, there's only one other place it will reside and that's in our own limited selves. We will be egocentric. Human beings *must* worship. Saint Francis said everything that exists is to be adored because God created it. So, Francis was in love with the God "out there" while being perfectly at home with the God shining through material creation.

This phrase of the Lord's Prayer is also saying that God is not nameable. The First and Second Commandments state that whatever word we use for God will be a metaphor (see Exodus 20:4–7). Don't use the name of God in vain. Don't use it lightly or easily, because it will never be adequate. So, keep the name holy. Use it delicately and with humility. The Hebrews didn't speak it at all because they knew whatever they spoke would be wrong. We would be much wiser had we learned some of that insight.

In some Hindu temples, worshipers walk through several courts and the inner court is absolutely empty. I saw the same in some Zen Buddhist temples in Japan, except with a twist: When you finally get to the inner court, there is simply a mirror. Both the Hindus and the Buddhists have a marvelous truth: When you finally get to the center, there's no name. You simply stand in the middle of the mystery. The middle court of the temple is usually dark too. *Holy* (*Kadosh*) literally means separate, beyond, too much, "far out."

"*Your kingdom come, your will be done on earth, as in heaven*" (Matthew 6:10): By saying, "your kingdom come," Jesus says we're inviting it into this world. We invite the eternal truth to happen now, in our midst on earth, as in heaven. That is the bridging of the great schism. What it means to live in the Reign of God is to live the final state of affairs now.

The first three petitions are for God's dominion in history and over us—a theocentric prayer that correctly realigns the order and keeps us out of the center.

If the first three petitions situate us correctly within the universe, the following four situate us as free people inside our own history: free to need God, to need one another, and to rely upon God's protection. Most people would consider that a freedom.

"*Give us today our daily bread. And forgive us our debts, as we have forgiven those who are in debt to us*" (Matthew 6:11–12): These phrases on bread and debts are clearly a prayer given to the poor. Bread and debt are the preoccupation, the entire life, of the peasant class. How do I have food for tomorrow and how do I pay my bills? In old English, the word was rendered as *trespasses*, which seems unchangeable now because we've said it for so long. But have no doubt about it: The word in the original text is clearly an economic word. Several of today's most respected Christian Scripture translations reflect that (*New Jerusalem* and *New Revised Standard Version*, for example).

We have spiritualized this petition, as we did most of the Gospel. We made this petition refer to private, individual forgiveness, about you trespassing against me, and it surely does have that meaning. But on the first level, this petition really refers to economic indebtedness. The power of this petition lies in the jubilee year, described in Leviticus 25:8–17. That's what Jesus is drawing upon. In ancient Israel, in every fiftieth year, everything went back to its original owner (see chapter eight). Ideally, all debts were forgiven. It was the great equalizer. It was a sign of the largesse and magnanimity of God.

If people had lived by the law of jubilee, communism would never have been necessary and capitalism would never have been possible. The spirit behind this jubilee thinking lasted for the first thousand years of Christianity, when someone could be excommunicated for taking interest on a loan (usury). The petition still raises questions about economics: How does the burden of debt—the personal debt people carry in our consumer society, the national debt carried particularly by low-income countries—keep people imprisoned in their own history?

Because of the economic meaning, Matthew 6:14–15, the warning to forgive others if we expect God to forgive us, was probably added to deal with personal sinfulness and forgiveness.

Asking for our daily bread is simply to trust that each day will take care of itself. What do the Twelve Step people say? One day at a time. That's what Jesus is saying here too. Don't live an anxious life of preparation for tomorrow.

In speaking of bread, Jesus is also building on the tradition of the manna. During the Exodus, the manna in the desert was only enough for the day. If they collected more than one day's worth, it would rot (see Exodus 16:4, 19–21). There's the symbolism: What we store up will rot. Living for today keeps us interdependent. *Daily* might be translated as "just enough," so we need God and one another to get through our days. That is surely on a course directly opposite from our culture, which prides itself on independence, self-sufficiency, personal control, and now shopping alone from home by TV or computer.

"And do not put us to the test, but deliver us from the Evil One" (Matthew 6:13): Our way of saying the same, perhaps, would be: "Make it easy for us, God. We are relying upon you because we can't do it by ourselves." Although this line is bothersome to many people because it seems to imply that God deliberately tests us, I think Jesus asked us to say it to realign ourselves with *what we need to trust*—that God will never lead us where God's love cannot sustain us. That is a great relief for anyone who has ever been led to the edge.

"Yes, if you forgive others their failings, your heavenly Father will forgive you yours; but if you do not forgive others, your Father will not forgive your

failings either" (Matthew 6:14–15): In case the disciples rejected the point about debts and the economic order, now, in the final verses of this section, Jesus does move it to the private order. It's the only petition that's repeated so we can't possibly miss the issue of forgiveness. I believe forgiveness is the whole Gospel: beginning, middle, and end.

Either/Or Language from a Both/And God

Like any good spiritual teacher, Jesus sums up his sermon by calling his listeners to a choice, or an "altar call," as the tent meetings would describe it. The options are set before us in very clear and decisive fashion. "Do you want the old world order, or do you want the new one that I have just described?" In a few verses, he will describe a series of paired options: two roads, two kinds of prophecy, two kinds of disciples, and two kinds of houses. There is no room for any in-between in Matthew's formulation of the Sermon.

Decisiveness is clearly seen as crucial to faith. Unless there is an organizing principle, unless there is one Lord, we will be lost in our own small world of preferences, interpretations, and cultural moods. We have no choice, it seems. We must place our bet. We must surrender to Another, or we will be subject to ourselves.

Russian philosopher Nikolai Berdyaev (1874–1948) put it very well: "Inner division wears away personality, and this division can be overcome only by making a choice, by selecting a definite object for one's love."[35] That definite object is, for us, the Reign of God and the person of Jesus.

Jesus describes the *two roads* as either "wide," leading to destruction, or "narrow" and "hard," leading to life. Many take the first, he says, and few find the second (see Matthew 7:13–14). The wide road that is taken by most is clearly a graphic description of what we would later call group-think, mimetic consciousness, and mob psychology—the ordinary and predictable paths of religious, economic, and political cultures. Left to ourselves, that is what we will likely do.

The narrow road is our new world order. Jesus has just described it for us and encourages us to take "the road less traveled." It is interesting that a book by that name has sold more than 3.5 million copies in the United States and 6.5 million worldwide—almost as if we know the common path is not the right one.

The *two kinds of prophets* or truth-speakers are to be discerned by one criterion: the kind of "fruit" that their lives create. Not, mind you, by their mild manner ("sheep's clothing") or even their claims about themselves ("a sound tree"), but by their final effect.

The old world order is built on a lie about the nature of reality. It allows us to use, exploit, and even destroy the divine image in other creatures. Any system that allows or even encourages us to objectify God's creatures for our own purposes is evil and will always produce evil fruit. Of course, this can never be seen from inside the system. Economic progress looks like progress when we are totally inside an economic culture. Listen to our people and our politicians as they unthinkingly accept this. Mere economic progress is only bad fruit from the criteria of the Reign of God. If we are blinded from inside the system, we will never see it. Thus, this simple criterion of "judge by the fruits" never felt very helpful to most people—and it isn't, unless we have already been blown away by the preceding sermon. If we have, we know exactly which fruit Jesus is speaking about.

The *two kinds of disciples* are also very telling. Jesus does not describe any ideal kind of creed or cult—but only a code of conduct. Jesus' emphasis is clearly on what we call *orthopraxy* (correct behavior or practice) over any kind of orthodoxy (correct thinking or opinion). To make this point, he even risks "offending pious ears," as we used to say: "It is not anyone who says to me, 'Lord, Lord,' who will enter the Reign of Heaven, but the person who does the will of my Father in heaven" (Matthew 7:21) that matters.

We who embrace the church traditions had better meditate on those lines for a long time. Why have we burned people at the stake for what they thought but hardly ever for what they did (unless it was an affront to churchly power)? Even better, why did we ever burn anybody at the stake at all?! Something got very mixed up here. It was still the old world order, hiding behind the glory of the new world order—and creating victims, as it always does. The old world order was, to use John's later description of Satan, "a murderer from the start; was never grounded in the truth…. [It] is a liar, and the father of lies" (John 8:44).

This description of Satan as the deceiver and murderer fits Matthew's understanding of the false way, the false teacher, and the false disciple. We can tell them all by their fruits: They will always be looking for victims to blame, exclude, and even kill. It is the litmus test of whether someone truly has the Spirit of God. Jesus, and his true disciples, have no need or desire to create victims. Jesus and his true disciples will not lie about God. God is good, and that good image is to be recognized and honored in all living things. It really is that simple. The old world order cannot accept such simplicity. The new world order can see nothing else.

The *two houses* are described as built either on sand or on rock (Matthew 7:24–27). Those who "listen" and "build" will not fall. Those who "listen" but "do not act on them" will be "stupid." They will fall, "and what a fall they will have."

Finally, Matthew has Jesus "sign" the document, after such a rousing conclusion, by describing him in a most unique way. There are *two kinds of authority* too: one, "like the scribes and Pharisees," needs to prop itself up by a reference or footnote to past religious authority or tradition, whereas Jesus' "teaching made a deep impression on the people because he taught with [inherent] authority" (see Matthew 7:28–29). He taught with a nonacademic, layperson's street wisdom, as we might say. It just rang true. It felt true. It was true, not because any authority said so, but because the Spirit confirmed it in the hearts of mature listeners. It is the same today.

The Foundation for the New World Order

In conclusion, allow me to give a simplified summary of what seems to be Jesus' foundational worldview and plan:

1) God is a God who can be trusted. God is like a loving "Father" who is involved in our lives and our world, so do not be afraid.

2). This God alone has the power to effect lasting and real change. Alignment with such truth is to live under the "Reign of God."

3) We are transformed to this Reign of God through a purifying journey into powerlessness and back. Jesus talked about it, then walked through it, and invited us to walk his Paschal Mystery ourselves.

4) Power unrefined by this journey into powerlessness will always be destructive and self-serving. It is unworthy of our loyalty or our hope. Therefore, we must:

    (a) Refuse our total allegiance ("idolatry") to all human systems of power, while still working around and even with them in a life of right relationship and service for justice.

    (b) Refuse to idolize or idealize the private self, which props itself up by myths of importance, control, and wealth.

    (c) Offer ourselves trustfully to a much larger pattern because *our lives are not about us.*

5) The motivation for all morality and religion is the imitation of God, who is love. When religion bases itself in fear, duty, honor, a need for law and order, a need for a superior self-image,

or group cohesiveness, it is corrupt. It looks good and will have many defenders, but it is actually at the heart of the problem. The real God is no longer needed or even wanted, and such religion usually becomes the actual enemy of God. The crucifixion of Jesus speaks to this.

6) This new world order, where love and power now work together, is seen by Jesus as a "wedding banquet." Meals seem to be his most constant image of what it is all about. Jesus seems to imply a world that is good, joy-filled, trustworthy, relational, communal, shared, and somehow, at the same time, local and small-scale—revolutionary on all points!

7) He teaches a style of listening and learning wisdom that emphasizes:

    (a) prayer of quiet and awareness,

    (b) social worship within a community and tradition,

    (c) reliance upon the Holy Spirit for guidance,

    (d) a wisdom that "will draw out from its storehouse things both old and new," and

    (e) a life of service to the suffering world—which is to imitate God.

epilogue

F_____ (1844–1900), a German philosopher and critic, _____ed the new world order that Jesus was teaching better than the vast majority of Christians. Unfortunately, he consciously chose against it. A genius in many ways, he saw the direction and the final significance of the Sermon on the Mount for human and European culture. He was convinced that culture needed myths of power and "heroism" to achieve what he saw as greatness. He declared that the teachings of Jesus would keep us like slaves and sheep.

Nietzsche rightly told his contemporaries that they were finally going to have to choose between this Jesus (who had already slowed them down) and the great mythic gods of Greece and Germany, which we now see are the tribal gods of economic, political, and religious cultures. In the twentieth century, many followed Nietzsche's advice, with disastrous consequences.

The twentieth century saw a succession of waves, each seeking dominance over the other, each seeing itself as the new and only answer. These waves were playing out the patterns that had already been given to us by the Enlightenment, the French and American Revolutions, and the Western philosophy of unlimited progress. It became modernism, which told us we could do it all, have it all, and explain it all.

When modernism appeared to fail, especially after the wars and holocausts of Christian nations, we fell into the present hopelessness called postmodernism. If reason, science, education, and technology cannot save us, then maybe there is no salvation. Maybe there are no universal patterns that are always true; maybe there is no beginning, middle, or end; maybe there are only private moments of meaning that we can grab from the universe. Even among many cultural Christians, the operative religion seems to be an official skepticism. If there is no Reign of God, we must live in a disenchanted and absurd world.

It is a time that feels like exile, in both our nations and our church. Cynicism comes too easily. Cynicism takes no surrender, no trust, no love, and no intelligence. It is no wonder so many of us hide there. It is too easy to dismiss whatever does not work *for us, right now,* especially if we think that our lives are about us.

Jesus has offered us a more spacious world, a world where we do not have to explain it, fix it, or control it; a world where we can allow a larger Mystery to work itself out through us and in us; a world where relationship is the beginning, the middle, and the end. It is, of course, still two worlds: the world as it is and the world as we now know it could be. One is founded in dominative power, and the other is a self-renewing call to right relationship. So many have tried, so many have given up, so many are pointing in other messianic directions. So many, even in the church, seem to have chosen power over love. Why should we keep proclaiming this Reign of God?

All I know is that Jesus proclaimed that Reign in a time of history when his people were dominated, discouraged, and enslaved; when religion was often corrupt; and when the number of people who understood were few. Yet he said, "The Reign of God is in your midst!" What is the alternative? Does anyone else have a greater wisdom or a greater vision? *To whom else shall we go?*

The more I preached around the world, the more I saw human history grinding down to a glacial freeze of remembered hurts, past oppressions, and family feuds that were held against one another unto the fourth and fifth generations. Now, with more efficient and effective research and history, we have even more convincing reasons to resent one another.

Everybody is a victim. Everybody can prove that they were oppressed somewhere. Everybody has a righteous grudge. Where do we find justice?

Unable to find justification in our minds or hearts, we go to courts of law, we seek vengeance and call it justice, we seek desperately for someone to blame because we are unhappy. Our unforgiveness leaves *us* prisoners as we guard the prison door of those we hate and fear. Even Christians seek from the law what was only promised us in the Spirit. We go to Caesar's house because Christ's stable seems so insecure. We have no home.

Fortunately, "Wisdom has built herself a house" (Proverbs 9:1). To live in this house of Wisdom is to let go of the past—and allow the future. To live in this house is to shake the dust from our feet—and live in a truly new way: the way of justice and mercy. It is all about forgiveness. Nothing new happens without forgiveness: the unmerited, the unnecessary, the totally gratuitous inbreaking of God into our systems of logic and culture.

Isn't that what God would likely do? Isn't that what we all need and desire? If this is not good news, *what* would be good news?

notes

CHAPTER ONE

1. I discuss this idea more fully in my book *A Lever and a Place to Stand: The Contemplative Stance, the Active Prayer* (New York: Paulist, 2011).

2. Martin Buber, *The Life of Dialogue*, 4th ed. (New York: Routledge, 2002), 65.

3. I want to acknowledge my gratitude to the important anthropological work of Gil Bailie (*Violence Unveiled*, Crossroad, 1995), and his own mentor, René Girard (*Violence and the Sacred*, Johns Hopkins University Press, 1979; *Things Hidden Since the Foundation of the World*, Stanford University Press, 1987). They have confirmed for me what Karl Rahner (1904–1984) always insisted, that for those of us from the Judeo-Christian tradition, theology and anthropology are the same thing. God is revealing who God is through human history and culture; the only God we know is the God we have met in our history.

4. Gil Bailie, *Violence Unveiled: Humanity at the Crossroads* (New York: Crossroad, 1995), 69.

5. George A. Panichas, ed., *The Simone Weil Reader* (Philadelphia: David McKay, 1977), 443.

CHAPTER TWO

6. John P. Meier, *A Marginal Jew: Rethinking the Historical Jesus* (New York: Doubleday, 1991), 331.

7. Dorothy Day, "Money and the Middle-Class Christian," *National Catholic Reporter*, February 18, 1970, as quoted in Brian Terrell, "Dorothy Day's 'filthy, rotten system' likely wasn't hers at all," *National Catholic Reporter*, April 16, 2012, https://www.ncronline.org/news/people/dorothy-days-filthy-rotten-system-likely-wasnt-hers-all.

CHAPTER THREE

8. Albert Nolan, *Jesus before Christianity*, rev. ed. (Maryknoll, NY: Orbis, 2001).

9. See *Dei Verbum*, the *Dogmatic Constitution on Divine Revelation* of the Second Vatican Council, especially chapters 1–3.

10. Robert G. Hamerton-Kelly, ed., *Violent Origins: Walter Burkert, René Girard, and Jonathan Z. Smith on Ritual Killing and Cultural Formation* (Stanford, CA: Stanford University Press, 1987), 141.

11. C. G. Jung, *Aion: Researches into the Phenomenology of the Self*, trans. R. F. C. Hull (Princeton, NJ: Princeton University Press, 1959), 44.

CHAPTER FOUR

12. John Dominic Crossan, *The Historical Jesus: The Life of a Mediterranean Jewish Peasant* (New York: HarperCollins, 1991).

13. Gerhard E. Lenski, *Power and Privilege: A Theory of Social Stratification* (New York: McGraw-Hill, 1966).

14. Thomas F. Carney, *The Shape of the Past: Models and Antiquity* (Lawrence, KS: Coronado Press, 1975), xiv.

15. Carney, *The Shape of the Past*, xiv.

16. Peter Wagner and Wendy Sawyer, "States of Incarceration: The Global Context 2018," *Prison Policy Initiative*, June 2018, https://www.prison-policy.org/global/2018.html.

CHAPTER FIVE

17. Crossan, *The Historical Jesus*, 341.

18. John Dominic Crossan, *Jesus: A Revolutionary Biography* (New York: HarperSanFrancisco, 1994), 121.

19. Gillian Feeley-Harnick, *The Lord's Table: Eucharist and Passover in Early Christianity* (Philadelphia: University of Pennsylvania Press, 1981), 10.

20. Lee Edward Klosinski, *The Meals in Mark* (Ann Arbor, MI: University Microfilms, 1988), 58.

21. Thomas Merton, *The Sign of Jonas* (New York: Harcourt, Brace, 1953), 362.

22. Kathy Coffey, *Hidden Women of the Gospels* (Maryknoll, NY: Orbis, 2003), 124–125.

23. Coffey, 124.

CHAPTER SEVEN

24. US Conference of Catholic Bishops, *Catechism of the Catholic Church* (New York: Doubleday, 1995), 538.

25. Jean Houston, *A Mythic Life: Learning to Live Our Greater Story* (New York: HarperCollins, 1996), 98.

26. Hamerton-Kelly, *Violent Origins*, 141.

CHAPTER EIGHT

27. Augustine of Hippo, *The Confessions of Saint Augustine*, Book I.

28. Richard Rohr, *Near Occasions of Grace* (Maryknoll, NY: Orbis, 1993), vii.

29. "Message of His Holiness Pope Paul VI for the Celebration of the Day of Peace, 1 January 1972," https://www.vatican.va/content/paul-vi/en/messages/peace/documents/hf_p-vi_mes_19711208_v-world-day-for-peace.html.

CHAPTER NINE

30. Charles Williams, *The Descent of the Dove: A Short History of the Holy Spirit in the Church* (Grand Rapids, MI: Eerdmans, 1939), 31.

31. Williams, 181.

32. Glen Stassen, *Just Peacemaking* (Louisville, KY: Westminster/John Knox, 1992).

33. *The Rule of the Third Order of Saint Francis for the Brothers and Sisters of the Order of Penitents*, paragraph 17, http://franciscanseculars. com/800-years-franciscan-third-order/.

34. "Address of His Holiness John Paul II to the 34th General Assembly of the United Nations," October 2, 1979, 17, https://www.vatican.va/ content/john-paul-ii/en/speeches/1979/october/documents/hf_jp-ii_ spe_19791002_general-assembly-onu.html.

35. Nicholas Berdyaev, *Dostoevsky* (New York: New American Library, 1974), 125.

About the Author

Richard Rohr is a globally recognized ecumenical teacher whose work is grounded in Christian mysticism, practices of contemplation and self-emptying, and compassion for the marginalized. He is a Franciscan priest of the New Mexico province and founder of the Center for Action and Contemplation in Albuquerque. Fr. Richard is the author of many books, including the bestsellers *Just This, What Do We Do with Evil?*, *The Universal Christ: How a Forgotten Reality Can Change Everything We See, Hope for, and Believe,* and *The Wisdom Pattern: Order, Disorder, Reorder.* The Center publishes Richard's Daily Meditations, free reflections emailed to hundreds of thousands around the world.